What They're Saying About
Medieval Underpants and Other Blunders

"I've been writing historical fiction for several decades, and I found this book immediately useful. I wish it had been published long ago. Written with humour, knowledge and common sense. An essential!"

Sandra Gulland, author, *Mistress of the Sun* & The Josephine B. Trilogy

"The single most useful book I've read on the craft of historical fiction. It's presented in a compulsively readable style that made it hard to put down. Riveting and beautifully logical, the book's mantra is never to assume you know something."

Jessica Knauss, author, *Law and Order in Medieval Spain*

"What a great idea, and so well done! . . . Best of all is the practical information and advice for avoiding errors that newbies need to consider and experienced writers need to remember. I can't say enough about this book. It was helpful; it was entertaining; it was original."

Peg Herring, author, The Simon & Elizabeth Mysteries and The Dead Detective Mysteries

Medieval Underpants

and

Other Blunders

A Writer's (& Editor's) Guide
to Keeping Historical Fiction
Free of Common Anachronisms,
Errors, & Myths

Second Edition

Susanne Alleyn

SPYDERWORT PRESS
ALBANY, NY

For further information, please contact Don
Congdon Associates, Inc., 110 William St., Suite
2202, New York, NY 10038, USA.
E-mail: dca@doncongdon.com

Second edition

ISBN-13: 978-1490424033

ISBN-10: 1490424032

10 9 8 7 6 5 4 3 2

The majority of illustrations used in this book,
including a few shamelessly borrowed from the
original edition of *Alice in Wonderland*, are
courtesy of WPClipart.com.

Spyderwort Press
Albany, NY, USA

Contents

Acknowledgments

hanks to all the fellow authors, editors, and fans of historical fiction, and readers of *Medieval Underpants and Other Blunders*, who sent me suggestions, corrections, priceless nuggets of information, pet peeves, and choice howlers they've come across in their own reading: including but not limited to Suzanne Adair, Albert Bell, Mari Bonomi, Margaret Chrisawn, Margaret Frazer, Peg Herring, Lin Jenkins, Martha Marks, Pat McIntosh, Nancy Means Wright, Meredith Phillips, Iva Polansky, Gev Sweeney, Sarah Waldock, and many other members of the Historical Fiction Authors Cooperative and CrimeThruTime who have shared their enthusiasm for history over the years. Keep the howlers coming!

Introduction

This is not a book on how to write historical fiction. There are many good books out there, including Persia Woolley's *How to Write and Sell Historical Fiction* and Kathy Lynn Emerson's *How to Write Killer Historical Mysteries*, that do an excellent job of that.

It *is* a book on how *not* to write historical fiction.

About a dozen years ago, when I was a member of a certain online discussion list for writers (published and unpublished) of historical fiction, a hopeful unpublished member posted some chapters of her work in progress, a romance set in 11th-century England, and asked for comments. I imagine she was naïvely eager to hear from other members about how good it was, and how they could hardly wait for her to finish it so that it would become an immediate bestseller.

Unfortunately, this poor soul proved to be a painfully, hopelessly bad writer, with a very shaky grasp of vocabulary, punctuation, and grammar. But even if she had been blessed with the most beautiful and perfect of writing styles, her complete lack of any realistic conception of life in the past, people's attitudes in past centuries, or indeed solid historical knowledge whatsoever would have doomed her; the extent of her historical study had probably been one book about the Norman Conquest and the not-very-attentive reading of a few third-rate bodice-ripper romances.

The ***first page*** of this writer's sample chapters included (this is supposed to be England in 1066, remember):

• A character lighting up a cigar [tobacco originated in the Americas, which, if it's slipped your mind, weren't discovered until 1492; and smoking cigars—rather than pipes—didn't really become popular until the 19th century.]

• Two characters chatting, while sitting on a leather sofa, in a roadside inn's cozy lounge [11th-century English roadside inns were not remotely cozy and had neither lounges nor leather-covered furniture; and no one in Western Europe had had anything like a sofa since the days of the Roman Empire.]

• One character casually mentioning that, since the coronation of King William [autumn 1066], he had just been on a trip to the Far East and had had a great time seeing China [two

centuries before Marco Polo spent years on his history-making journey from Venice to China and back, and when a traveler was lucky if he covered forty miles a day—did this fellow get to China, and back to England, *within two months* by going to Travelocity.com and buying a discounted airfare?]

• One character greeting another with "You look great." [Ouch. Just ouch.]

There were probably many more hideous howlers of this sort, but (thankfully) I've forgotten them . . .

Most anachronisms and errors in published historical fiction, from now on to be referred to as "HF", aren't this obvious or ludicrous. But plenty do crop up, and many common errors keep on reappearing from book to book to book because inexperienced writers (and sometimes even experienced writers and their editors) haven't done their homework properly.

We HF writers all make mistakes. None of us has lived in ancient Rome or 11th-century England or 19th-century America and we can't possibly know every single detail of events and everyday life and what a person living in such an era would take for granted. There's probably not a historical novel anywhere that doesn't have some errors or anachronisms in it, whether teensy weensy or so painfully obvious that you wonder what the editor was smoking to have missed them. I've made a few mistakes that ended up in my own published novels. But I've caught them in the end (or other people did) and I sure won't make those particular mistakes again.

The teensy weensy mistakes are the ones that (thank goodness) will only be caught by the handful of scholarly experts across the entire globe who have made a career out of that particular obscure subject. If you mention, as I did in my own novel *The Cavalier of the Apocalypse*, the Montansier Theater in Paris in 1786, probably only people who have advanced degrees in the history of late-18th-century French theater are ever going to catch that and snicker briefly because they remember that the real Montansier Theater in Paris—as opposed to the Montansier Theater in Versailles—wasn't founded until 1790.

Oops.

Yes, I was careless and goofed there with a tiny, unimportant detail that had nothing to do with the plot. (Oh, well, I'll fix it in the next edition.)

The big, honking, obvious howlers, however, are the ones that no self-respecting author/researcher should commit and no editor should let him get away with—though they often do.

"Never mind," the amateur writer thinks, when she gives her knight a cigar without wondering whether or not people smoked cigars in the 11th century, because she's much more interested in describing the effect of the heroine's sex appeal on the hero's "manhood": "Nobody will notice."

"Never mind," the professional writer thinks, when he's describing the food at Emperor Marcus Aurelius's banquet, but is too busy or lazy to look up the histories of individual foods and find out whether or not tomato and basil salad dressed in olive oil (a nice modern Italian dish) could actually have been served there. "Nobody will notice."

Yes, they will.

Some people *will* notice.

Some people who know their history *will* know that tobacco was unknown in medieval Europe and that tomatoes couldn't possibly have been part of an ancient Roman banquet, and now the author's just set himself up with them as a sloppy researcher whose historical details (and who knows what else?) can't be trusted.

If you dress your aristocratic ancient Roman heroine in a toga, for instance, or give her a dinner involving tomatoes, just about anybody who has studied ancient Rome—or even anybody who has read a lot of (more reliable) historical fiction about ancient Rome—will say "Whaaaat?"

Because before you write your Roman novel, you'd better have learned at least enough about ancient Roman life to know that only men wore togas, and enough about world history and food history to know that tomatoes originated in Central America and didn't make it to Europe, Africa, and Asia until the 1500s (A.D.) at the very earliest. Displaying this kind of ignorance about fairly basic facts will, most likely, get your book tossed across the room by 95% of its readers, who love ancient Rome and read lots of HF about ancient Rome and have picked up lots and lots of details about life in ancient Rome, and now you've just proved that you know less than they do and your historical research is not to be relied upon.

This guide is intended to point out, remind you about, and help you keep your historical fiction free of, not only the big honking howlers, but also the many, many lesser gaffes and howlers that keep turning up again and again in all kinds of HF written by authors who should know better. Its focus is primarily toward European/American history, since my own specialized knowledge is centered in Europe and the 18th century in particular, and the great majority of historical fiction written in English is set in Europe, the Europeanized Americas, or the ancient Mediterranean. Many topics here, however, can be applied on a broader scale to fiction set in other cultures, regions, and eras. Babylonian ziggurat builders and 14th-century Japanese samurai, after all, didn't have cigars or tomatoes any more than 11th-century English knights did.

I am also writing from an American perspective and primarily for North American readers and writers, but I hope readers from other nations will enjoy this book, find it useful, and not take offense.

May we never again read about Dark Ages peasants eating tomatoes; unbelievably plucky/feisty, liberated medieval heroines with names like Dominique; 18th-century travelers crossing Europe or the Atlantic in a week and a half; slang that's sixty years ahead of its time; and many, many other such common anachronisms of fact and attitude . . .

Onward!

Basic Rules
You Need To Keep In Mind
That Will Help You Avoid
the Silly Mistakes

General Rule
No. 1

Never Assume

There's an old wisecrack that goes: "Never assume something, because when you assume, you make an *ass* out of *u* and *me*."

This is especially true of writing and researching historical fiction.

Never assume anything about the details of historical events or daily life in the past!

Look it up!

1

Anachronisms

"**Anachronism**: (from the Greek *ana* [up, against, back, re-] and *chronos* [time]) A chronological inconsistency in some arrangement, especially a juxtaposition of person(s), events, objects, or customs from different periods of time.

"A *prochronism* occurs when an item appears in a temporal context in which it could not yet be present (the object had not yet been invented, the verbal expression had not been coined, the philosophy had not been formulated, the technology had not been created, etc.)."

adapted from Wikipedia

nachronisms, or, to be exact, prochronisms, make up most of the howlers in HF. I've already given a few examples of things that show up in historical novels that could not possibly have appeared as the authors state they did, simply because they are decades or centuries ahead of their time. I'll continue to discuss the most common anachronisms that are forever turning up in HF because inexperienced authors don't do enough basic research, and because experienced authors don't always take the time to ask themselves, "Wait a minute—am I *quite* sure that this item, building, technology, street, expression, attitude, food, or custom actually existed in the period and place I'm writing about?"

In other words, they mistakenly *assume* . . .

2

Let's Start With the Underpants

(This section mentions slightly indelicate subjects.
You've been warned.)

rdinary men in the Middle Ages wore underpants, of a sort. They were called *braies* or *breeks* and they were of plain linen gathered together at the waist, rather like a cross between a loose loincloth and baggy breeches, all held in place by a belt.

But the simplest thing to remember about *women*'s underwear in past eras is this: They probably weren't wearing any.

This is not to say that wealthy, aristocratic European women didn't wear anything beneath their elaborate court gowns. Of course they did. But the "body linen" that they wore would have looked much more like the knee-length T-shirts that many of us sleep in than anything ever dreamed up in the Victoria's Secret catalogue.

Through most of history, if European women wore an undergarment, it was a plain, short-sleeved affair that fell to between the knees and the ankles—possibly gathered with stitching and/or a drawstring under the breasts to provide a little support—of soft linen (not cotton!). In English it was called a smock (early Middle Ages), a shift (Middle Ages through 18th century), or a chemise or "shimmy" (in the 19th century, adopted from the French). If the woman wore a corset, it went on over the shift so that the wearer's skin wasn't chafed from the hard bones of the corset.

The corset gave you a fashionably narrow waist but did little to improve your bosom—there was nothing like a bra as part of it. Most corsets, over the centuries, either stopped below the breasts and let the shift and gown do the work of supporting them, or, if the corset went higher, it held the bosom in place by simply pushing it inward and, inevitably, somewhat upward. (And corsets, until the late 19th century, the tail end of the Age of the Corset, were plain and functional, more like a 1950s girdle, their descendant, than anything else—they weren't red or black or trimmed with lace, no matter how they may remind you of a sexy teddy from the local "naughty undies" shop.)

And what kind of panties did the pre-19th-century woman wear with her shift?

She didn't.

A lot of beginning authors probably have the idea . . . gathered from movies, no doubt . . . that women throughout the ages wore lacy underdrawers or pantalettes or bloomers of some sort as an undergarment for their nether regions. Costume movies, which are particularly guilty of this anachronism, are rife with ladies' ruffled bloomers in all centuries (see General Rule No. 3, *Do Not Borrow Your Information From Other People's Historical Novels and Movies*); the moviemakers have to put *something* on their curvaceous stars, after all, for the sake of the PG rating. Movies probably give their heroines pantalettes in a caught-in-her-underwear scene because they look sexier than a petticoat. But unless it's the middle of the 19th century or later, the drawers rarely belong there.

Until the mid 1800s, it's likely that most Western women

didn't wear anything resembling modern underpants, whether drawers or briefs—unless, perhaps, it was That Time of the Month, when a snug loincloth, holding some rags or other absorbent material in place, was undoubtedly welcome. Why?

Well, the rough date when women began to wear modern underpants (meaning loose drawers, and then—*considerably* later, well after World War I—snug briefs/panties) corresponds, not coincidentally, with the early development of the modern toilet and the modern public toilet—the middle of the 19th century—and also with more liberating female clothing and modern notions of privacy. [1]

Imagine that you're a 13th-century peasant woman on your way to the fields or the market, and that you need to relieve yourself. Do you really want to go behind a tree and squat, and then reach under your heavy woolen skirts and your shift and hitch them up, inevitably exposing yourself to any companions or passersby, in order to untie (no elastic waistbands, remember) and pull down your bloomers or panties?

Imagine that you are wearing a late Elizabethan court gown with a farthingale the size of a cart wheel, or a 1770s ball gown with five-foot-wide panniers, and that you need to relieve yourself. Do you really want to squat over a chamber pot while wearing that gown, and then try to reach underneath yards of fabric and the elaborate wicker or whalebone or metal framework of your hoops or panniers, *plus* some petticoats, *plus* your shift, in order to untie and pull down your bloomers or panties?

I didn't think so. (And any actress or Civil War reenactor who's worn 21st-century underwear beneath a bulky period gown plus petticoats and hoops would probably agree.)

Without the underdrawers, you just hunker down and spread your skirts and whiz. So much easier and so much more modest (though the lack of underpants also made quick sexual encounters up against a wall a lot easier). That's how women

---

[1] For a brief, entertaining essay on the possibility or impossibility of relieving oneself as seen in Victorian fiction, see John Sutherland, "Why are there no public conveniences in Casterbridge?" in *Who Betrays Elizabeth Bennet? Further Puzzles in Classic Fiction* (Oxford University Press, 1999).

relieved themselves for millennia, even in civilizations like ancient Rome that had toilets at "sitting" height; ancient Roman public latrines seem to have been unisex because both genders simply sat and spread their clothing decently over themselves while they were tending to their business. (For cleaning up, they used a damp sponge on the end of a stick—the holes in the vertical part of the toilet benches are where you'd poke the stick. Nasty, sycophantic sidekick characters in Roman farces thus were often nicknamed "Sponge.")

The very *concept* of women wearing underpants—garments similar to, and performing the same function as, trousers or breeches, which were worn by *men*—offended some people. When Catherine de' Medici (queen and dowager queen of France 1547-1589) introduced a type of female underbreeches, called *calçon*, which were specifically intended for the comfort and modesty of women riding horseback in case their skirts flew up during a hard gallop, her younger contemporaries welcomed them as a useful innovation but certain moralists were shocked: "Beneath her skirts," one declared, "a woman's ass should be naked as God intended."[2]

Over 200 years later, Benjamin Franklin, when American minister to France, apparently had a strategic view of a lady in waiting who took a disastrous spill in the palace. He remarked to Marie-Antoinette on the interesting fact that the aristocratic ladies at Versailles—who wore some of the most cumbersome court gowns in history—didn't wear underdrawers of any sort and that "the gates of Paradise [were] always open." (It's possible that women in Franklin's 18th-century America, which had no big court gowns and was a lot more strait-laced—and colder in the winter—than most of 18th-century Europe, had already adopted drawers, with warmth and modesty trumping convenience.) A decade later, during the French Revolution, eyewitnesses recounted that when Marie-Antoinette was about to climb into the cart that

---

[2] Quoted in Guy Breton, *Histoires d'Amour de l'Histoire de France*, vol. II. The vulgarity (*cul*, "ass") is in the original 16th-century French.

would take her to the guillotine, she suddenly asked the executioner to untie her hands, so that she could relieve herself. Keeping it simple with an absence of panties, she slipped into a corner of the prison courtyard, crouched, spread her skirts, and did her business, before proceeding with the journey.

Detail of caricaturist Thomas Rowlandson's "The Exhibition Staircase" (1811), in which obese but fashionable Londoners tumble down a notoriously steep stairway; it's abundantly clear that the ladies aren't wearing drawers.

Very recent archeological finds at a castle in the Austrian Tyrol (eastern Alps) reveal the existence of—yes—medieval bras and something that could be "underpants"—but we have no way of knowing how often they were worn.

We have to remember that the situation usually determines the solution, and people tend to invent and use the things that are most useful to them. Bras or other kinds of boob-repressors are welcome things to big-breasted women in any place and at any time. A woman with an oversize bosom in any century would have come up with some sort of binding to keep her breasts in place, though not necessarily the very modern-looking "bikini bra" discovered at Lengberg (less modern-looking items used for the same purpose were called in the Middle Ages, unflatteringly, "shirts with bags").

The underpants are trickier. The discovery in a castle of two pairs of 15th-century panties (actually snug loincloths more resembling string bikini bottoms, with a few inches of ribbon or tape at the sides for tying together) does not mean, by a long shot, that everyone wore them. It's most likely that they were used only when their owner had her period, for the sake of keeping that absorbent padding in place; there's not much of a reason for their existence otherwise. But we just don't know. And still we have to go back to the whole question of *convenience.*

Recall: Why didn't 16th-, 17th-, and 18th-century aristocratic women wear underpants? Because of the insane *in*convenience that would have been involved in reaching around and below their enormous, heavy, boxy gowns and frames and petticoats to untie the ribbons on the Lengberg undies, versus the ease and simplicity of sitting or squatting pantless over a chamber pot. 15th-century gowns, on the other hand, were much simpler in their lines, with flowing skirts and few underskirts, and didn't have the bulky frameworks that Renaissance and Early Modern formal clothing did.

Why didn't peasant women wear underpants? Because peasants and poor town workers had no privies and practically no privacy. Peasant women and working-class women, when they had to take a leak in the middle of the work day, weren't about to hunt for a private, sheltered place—if they could find one at all—in which they could hike up their skirts in peace; it was far more convenient and modest to walk a few steps from where they were working, whether the middle of the field or their own cottages or the marketplace, and squat pantless on the ground, with their bodies and their bodily functions respectably hidden by their skirts.

The Lengberg Castle underpants—*if* they were for everyday use and not just once-a-month accessories—were evidently worn by a woman who had neither of these problems. She would have been wearing the relatively simple skirt of the 15th century, and she was undoubtedly an aristocrat with easy access to the castle privy, garderobe shaft, or chamber pot hidden behind a discreet screen. She would have had the privacy to relieve herself in peace, away from rude stares, and would have worn a gown that was fairly easy to reach under in order to untie her string panties. The vast majority of women of her own time would not have had the same privacy; while upper-class women of subsequent centuries who did have the privacy would been hampered by their dresses.

In the end, it comes down to the simple fact that we use what works best for us. And if underpants are both convenient and necessary, as they are today when Western women wear either short skirts or trousers, we wear them; if, beneath heavy, voluminous skirts, underpants are *in*convenient and *un*necessary, we don't.

So how were modern underpants eventually adopted?

The first pantalettes, dating from the 1810s, weren't actually the underdrawers we'd *assume* they were. They were merely a leg covering and decorative affectation for girls (and very young boys, who customarily wore dresses until any age between two and eight), made to hang below the hem of a child's relatively short calf-length skirts. They were no more than a pair of separate fabric tubes, though, with trimming at the bottom, that were tied to the waistband at each side of the hips like medieval hose, or to the leg over the knee with drawstrings or garters, and weren't in any way bloomers or trouserlike. (Next page: a little girl wearing long, ankle-length pantalettes in an engraving from the 1810s.)

Convenient crotchless underwear of this sort was popular for several decades in the 19th century—for the usual bathroom reasons, not for the reasons that spring to mind when we eye the split-crotch red satin teddies in the window of the Pink Pussycat. The idea (after Catherine de' Medici's riding underpants were swept away by history) that leg coverings could envelop *all* of a woman's lower torso, like trousers, developed with improvements in indoor plumbing and the chance to use it in privacy—in the mid 19th century—along with the slow evolution of less cumbersome female garments.

Paradoxically, the hoopskirt of the 1850s and 60s was also one of the reasons women started adopting more trouser-like undergarments, because the mid-19th-century hoopskirt or cage crinoline, unlike the gowns of earlier centuries that were made of heavy fabrics and relied on multiple layers of petticoats to fill them out, was comparatively mobile. A gust of wind could get under a wide hoop framework and light petticoat and summer gown (both petticoat and gown often made of cotton, which was fashionable, lightweight, and inexpensive) and blow the whole arrangement inside-out like a flyaway beach umbrella, with highly embarrassing results. If a lady, moreover, forgot to hitch her hoops up and behind her a little when sitting down, the result was a slapstick moment—the front of her gown would flip upward and, if she was really unlucky, hit her on the nose while giving spectators a free show. Whether or not women found the concealing modesty of wearing underdrawers beneath their chemises worth the inconvenience of trying to relieve themselves while wrestling with their hoops is debatable.

Peasants and the urban poor, on the other hand, whose

best opportunity for decently relieving themselves in public was probably to crouch over a gutter (already reeking with manure from livestock) and spread their skirts, were probably going without what we'd think of as underpants (snug briefs) for as long as women wore ankle-length dresses: in other words, at least until World War I or so, and possibly into the 1920s or even 30s with older women, and/or in isolated and backward areas of Europe and the Americas. (My grandfather could tell us of his own childhood memories of seeing peasant women in northeastern Germany—circa 1905—squatting over the gutter at the market, skirts spread. My American grandmother, meanwhile, born in 1894, stuck with loose knee-length drawers in a pattern fashionable in the 1920s, one that today we'd think of as a split slip rather than as "panties"; she was uncomfortable with, and simply didn't wear, slacks or pantsuits even in the 1970s, and probably never wore modern briefs in her life.) It's a relatively safe bet that until women began to regularly wear short skirts, mid-calf or higher—less than a hundred years ago—and then at last to wear trousers, which would chafe without them, women's briefs were simply an unnecessary item of clothing except during their monthly periods.

No, you don't need to mention in your novel, if you don't want to, that your 14th-century or Regency heroine isn't wearing underdrawers or anything else of the panty persuasion. But, for the love of Mike—unless your story is set after 1840-ish—when your hero and heroine start tearing each other's clothes off at the beginning of an exciting scene, don't start in on a full description of the lady's lacy bloomers.

And, by the way . . .

Both American and British speakers of the English language say "underpants" to refer to what's under our trousers, ***BUT***: keep in mind that in modern Britain, "underpants" are a man's garment—women wear "knickers" or "pants" or "panties" or simply "underwear." More important still, American writers who set stories in the British Isles—or, indeed, who hope to have British readers of anything they write—*must* keep in mind that **British people do NOT use the word "pants" to mean anything but "underwear"**! If you describe your English duke's "pants" when you should really be speaking of his trousers, particularly in a historical novel, you're going to have a lot of British readers laughing hysterically.

Aside: Why wouldn't our ancient or medieval or Tudor lady wear a cotton shift?

Because linen is Middle Eastern and cotton is Asian. Flax can grow in a cold climate and Europeans have been making linen from it for thousands of years. Cotton, on the other hand, originally came from the Indian subcontinent and needs a warm climate to grow in.

Cotton cloth, a light, cool fabric that took dyes or prints easily, only grew popular in Europe as an expensive import (from India) in the mid to late 1700s. It only grew *cheap* in Europe in the early 1800s when (a) the cotton gin was invented (which vastly speeded up the processing of raw cotton), thus suddenly making cotton a very profitable crop for the Americans, who planted it all over the warm Southern states; and (b) the British began importing cotton for their cloth mills from the United States rather than from much-more-distant India. (Disruptions in the cotton exports during the U.S. Civil War eventually led to cotton being planted in Egypt, which started the modern Egyptian cotton trade. But no ancient Egyptian ever wore cotton—all their clothes, bed-sheets, and mummy wrappings were of linen.)

And that's why we still say "household linens" today when referring to the bed sheets and towels and other contents of our "linen cupboard," even though 95% of what's in there today is probably cotton or cotton/poly rather than actual linen.

Aside #2: What about, um, chastity belts?

Chastity belts are a myth.

(You're not suggesting that women who, for the sake of

convenience, wouldn't even have regularly worn cloth undies would have chosen to wear *metal* ones, are you???)

If anything of the sort ever did exist, a woman probably wore it intentionally—for a very short term, a day or two at best—to prevent rape. The hygienic consequences of long-term wear of anything large and stiff enough in the crotch to balk a rapist (or a seducer) would have been appalling. Fecal infections, especially via the chafing sores that would have soon developed in such a sensitive area of the body, would have killed a wearer pretty quickly in an era without toilet paper, disinfectants, or antibiotics. Any "chastity belts" you may see in medieval museums are most likely fakes from later centuries, hoaxes created to titillate gawkers in 18th- and 19th-century "cabinets of curiosities."

Just try wearing one.

3

Anachronisms in Locations: Getting the Geography Right

If you've decided to set your period novel in a fictional English or American town or a small imaginary Balkan kingdom, then you don't need to worry about getting your streets right. If, however, you're setting your story in London, Paris, New York, or any major city worldwide, or even a smaller town that happens to have an active historical society, and you plan to be the least bit specific about your locations, the first thing you need—even if you live there—is a map.

But don't run to the travel section in the nearest Barnes & Noble or WH Smith and grab a dumbed-down tourist map of Paris or Rome (*"Nobody will notice . . ."*). If you do that, you're setting yourself up for a whole lot of howlers.

Most people know, or can figure out, that very old cities usually consist of concentric rings of growth; the oldest part of the city is in the center, usually at a strategic point on the banks of a river, and the buildings grow newer as they are built farther and farther out from the center, except where the growing cities gobble up equally old villages or small towns in their path. (New York City's center is not so much its rivers as its harbor; the longest-settled parts of Manhattan and

Brooklyn are by the waterfront.) What many authors don't realize, however, is that cities—both large and small—don't just grow outward; they can change internally, especially if they are capital cities and their rulers are determined on making showplaces of their capitals. So avenues are continually being built, pierced through areas that previously may have had only tiny, narrow, medieval streets; grand squares are set down at the intersections of avenues; large public building projects or urban rebuilding can demolish and take the place of decrepit, dangerous neighborhoods; streets frequently change their names to commemorate monarchs, cultural celebrities, and events.

Though all cities have their pitfalls, the easiest major city to get wrong in HF is probably Paris. There are any number of under-researched historical novels set in 17th- or 18th-century Paris in which people are walking along streets that were not even in existence until decades or centuries later.

If your historical novel is set in Paris after 1900, then you're mostly safe with a modern map (while always remembering that the Musée d'Orsay was originally a train station, that the Centre Pompidou wasn't begun until 1971 and the Opéra Bastille until 1984, that the Forum des Halles used to be a wholesale meat and produce market with 19th-century iron pavilions, not a park and underground shopping mall, and that the outer edge of the city will not have been at all the same a hundred or more years ago . . . OK, maybe you need that 1921 map after all)—as long as you look up *every single street name*, because the Parisians just love to rename their streets, particularly in honor of their heroes, cultural figures, or important events. You can be sure, for instance, that Avenue Franklin

D. Roosevelt and Place du 18 Juin 1940 were called something else in 1900.

(French Wikipedia, if you can read French, is excellent for this because it has an individual web page for just about every street in Paris, which often includes previous names of the street and the date of the street's creation: do a search for your street, beginning with "Rue" or "Boulevard" or whatever, at http://fr.wikipedia.org/ .)

Paris before 1870, however, is a lethal minefield for the author of HF, owing mostly to the efforts of two people: Emperor Napoleon III and Baron Eugène Haussmann, the prefect of the city. Napoleon III and Haussmann transformed Paris from a medieval/Renaissance city full of narrow, serpentine streets and alleys, its longest and straightest streets dating back to Roman times, to a modern, 19th-century one streamlined by straight, broad avenues and boulevards. They ran some of the new wide streets straight through ancient neighborhoods, demolishing buildings and shortening, widening, or obliterating many old streets in the process. As a result of this, the glamor of Paris is mostly from the late 19th century and genuine, mostly untouched, 17th- and 18th-century neighborhoods are harder to find. The city of Bordeaux, which got the massive rebuilding treatment a hundred years earlier, now looks a lot more like 18th-century Paris than Paris does (as French filmmakers know; it stands in for Paris in a lot of period movies).

So Paris, between 1851 and 1870, lost a lot of small streets and gained a fair number of grand avenues—and made it so perilously easy for an author without the right map and with too many assumptions to tell us, as one very well-known historical author does, about a 1792 character standing at the corner of the Boulevard St. Germain—which didn't exist until 1855. (In another French Revolution novel, set in 1793, the same author manages to compound the error by mentioning not only the Boulevard St. Germain but also the Boulevard St. Michel—which was not pierced through the Left Bank until the 1860s. Can it not have occurred to this otherwise meticulous author that a late-18th-century map of Paris would come in useful?)

Though, to be fair, even the French goof badly sometimes: a modern French literary novel about the Revolution has someone in 1794 looking out a window at Rue de Rivoli, which was named after what a French author of HF really should have known was one of Napoleon's victories in 1797, for gosh sakes—and the street itself didn't exist until 1806. And perhaps the very worst map anachronism *ever* has to be the mentioning of the Via Cavour, a street in Rome, in a novel set during the reign of Augustus, in the first century B.C.; the Count of Cavour, the first prime minister of modern Italy, was born in 1810, somewhat after Augustus's time.

In short: No matter what city or town you're describing, buy, beg, borrow, or steal; download, photocopy, or scan, any way you know how, a period map from as close as possible to the year you're writing about. Historical museums' book shops (in major cities) or local historical societies (in smaller towns) can often provide these, or help you find one.

Having the right map from the right time grows more and more important the farther back you go. While Paris in

1790 didn't look anything like Paris in 1890, Paris in 1590 looked even less like it. The picture on the previous page is of Philadelphia in the early 18th century; it looks a little different now. And a street at the edge of London in 1815 may not have existed as anything more than a cowpath through rural fields in 1780—or may not have existed at all.

You don't even have to be writing about one of the world's major capitals to get streets wrong—and to have an eagle-eyed local historian gently correct you—as one author found out after using a 1790-ish map to find the names of streets in 17*80*-ish Wilmington, North Carolina. So when you're looking for a period map, if you can't find one made in exactly the year you're writing about, it's better to get hold of a map created slightly *before* your story's date rather than after—if you still get a street name wrong, it's just a little less embarrassing to mention a street (which had been renamed two years before) and use its former name than to use a name that didn't yet exist.

4

Ånachronisms & Bloopers In Dialogue, Expressions, & Slang

"Yea, Verily, 'Tis a Bad Hair Day"

ne of the difficulties authors of HF must face is the problem of how their characters talk. If an American author is writing a historical novel set in New York City in 1925, then she has fewer worries, since everybody's speaking English to begin with and people used pretty much the same speech patterns and basic vocabulary, ninety years ago, as they do today—no one would mistake, by his speech, a New Yorker from 1925 for a New Yorker from 1725.

Authors writing a novel set in ancient Egypt or in 15th-century Italy, on the other hand, face a double problem: they're writing dialogue that would actually have been in another language entirely, and, moreover, often the dialogue is set in an alien time period in which the slang and common idiomatic expressions would have been completely untranslatable. And if authors aren't careful, blatantly 21st-century expressions can creep in, land with a resounding *thud*, and make a 15th-century dialogue seem ludicrous.

You don't need a five- or ten-century difference for this

to cause a problem, either. Slang and idiomatic expressions pop up suddenly and can hang around for hundreds of years, or disappear within a decade. (Most expressions, what's more, have stayed on their own side of the Atlantic until the 1970s or so, when American TV shows became popular in the U.K. and vice versa, and Americanisms and Britishisms started to slip into each other's vernacular . . . though the classic Americanism "O.K." has been employed in Britain since the 1920s, probably picked up during World War I).

Your 1925 New York flapper may have said "Twenty-three skiddoo!" or "It's simply the bee's knees," but you can bet your boots that her daughter never used either of those expressions in 1940 or 1950—nor did her British cousin at any time, even 1925. (Read any of P.G. Wodehouse's hilarious novels or stories written in the 1920s for countless examples of the slangy speech of upper-class twentysomethings (the Bright Young Things) in Jazz Age Britain—it's as distinctive as the enhanced California teen slang in *Buffy the Vampire Slayer*.) Nor would your 1925 New Yorker ever say she was "having a bad hair  day" or tell anyone to "get a life"—those expressions wouldn't appear for another sixty years—any more than a 2013 New Yorker would say something was "groovy" or "far out" (late 1960's, in case you weren't around then) unless she was being deeply, self-consciously ironic.

Before you put an idiomatic phrase in the mouth of a character, even one who's speaking modern (i.e. mid-19th-century or later) English, *look it up*. You may not need to "translate" your dialogue from a foreign language or from Renaissance English—but you do need to watch, like a hawk, that you don't unthinkingly put an expression evocative of

2010 or 1995 or 1970 into the mouth of your 1650 character—or even your 1950 character. Look it up: Somewhere in a book or the Internet you'll find out when a popular expression became popular and when it began to fade. And if you grew up saying "bad hair day" but don't have a clue that nobody ever said "bad hair day"—or "have a clue" or "clueless," for that matter—before 1990 or so, then you need to read fiction and plays published in, and/or watch movies made in (that's "made *in*," not "made *about*"—see General Rule No. 3, *Do Not Borrow Your Information From Other People's Historical Novels and Movies*), the decades you're writing about and develop an instinctive ear for what they said and, even more important, what they *didn't* say.

Otherwise you'll end up with painfully anachronistic nonsense, such as the multiple gaffes that turn up in a much overrated American novel, *Mr. Churchill's Secretary*, set in World War II London. This book's numerous, anachronistic dialogue howlers and the gratuitous, fifty-years-ahead-of-its-time political correctness incessantly spouted by the tiresome, self-righteous heroine unfortunately made it past a history-challenged editor at a big NYC publishing house.

The author, while adequately researching the events and tangible details of everyday life in wartime England, obviously didn't watch nearly enough 1930s/40s movies or read enough Agatha Christie or Evelyn Waugh or other British pre-war novelists to get a grip on the sound of the time and place, for she doesn't have the vaguest idea how the British, or even Americans, spoke in the 1940s. (Even the novel's *title* is inaccurate and smacks of an American taint—the British term for the heroine's office job would have been simply "typist"; "secretary" implied something quite different from what she's doing in the story.) The characters, American and British both, continually use 1990s and 2000s American expressions and speech patterns (not coincidentally, the decades in which the author apparently grew up), employing such trendy, anachronistic monstrosities as "He was tight with Ambassador Kennedy."

Yuck!

This line, for anyone with an ear for dialogue, is just as cringeworthy an anachronism as having Winston Churchill whip out his iPhone. Somehow this thirtysomething author was completely unaware that the Americanism "He's tight with X" didn't come to mean "he's friendly/intimate with X" until five decades after World War II—and, what's more, that "tight," in genuine, commonly used British and American slang of the first half of the 20th century, actually meant "tipsy" or "drunk." (The context of the fictional conversation clearly shows us that the author meant "intimate" and not "intoxicated.")

What was the author (or her editor) *thinking*?

Of course, sometimes an author chooses to write his historical novel using consciously modern slang, casual language, and speech patterns, with the valid arguments that every period in time is "modern" to the people who are living in it, and that people have always spoken casually rather than sounding like the often formal, mannered dialogue of plays from the period. (Look at Shakespeare's use of informal, ordinary prose speech with his comic lower-class and servant characters—it's rich and slangy and vulgar and very "real," as opposed to the beautiful, poetic, but not at all realistic dialogue of his aristocratic heroes.)

This choice, to roughly approximate another era's and language's slangy idioms in a 20th/21st-century, British or American, informal style, is best used with a (usually urban) setting that could parallel hip 21st-century life, and in which we're suspending our disbelief and pretending that no one is actually speaking any form of English. I'd strongly recommend you not try this with trendy Elizabethans or Georgians, for example, when we know pretty well (from contemporary dramatists and novelists) how ordinary Englishmen or American colonists in the 16th or 18th centuries actually talked. Lindsey Davis and David Wishart, on the other hand, both carry the concept off well—although the deliberately modern, Raymond Chandler-esque style annoys some readers—in their respective mysteries set in ancient Rome—a hip, fast-paced, gritty urban setting that could indeed parallel 21st-century New York City, L.A., or London:

> "I need a favour from you, Corvinus. Do what Occusia asks, and I'll be very grateful. Very grateful indeed. Turn her down, or fudge things, and—watch my lips here, please—you'll wish that you'd never been born. Your choice, absolutely no pressure. You understand?"
>
> [from *No Cause for Concern* by David Wishart]

If you choose to deliberately use modern-sounding casual dialogue, you'll need to proceed very, very carefully in order not to produce something ludicrous—most likely by using a bit of current 21st-century slang that works in 2013 but may sound laughably dated in another ten or twenty years. Choosing casual, slangy language that has a relatively "timeless" quality about it—something like "fudge things" or "no pressure" that could have been used any time during the past fifty years, rather than being extremely and absurdly typical of a particular decade, including one's present decade—is best. (Yes, you'll still have to do your homework to be certain that an expression you're using doesn't date only from 2004.)

Here are a couple of examples from my own works, using casual dialogue and narration, in which we're pretending that everyone is actually speaking colloquial 18th-century French:

[from *A Treasury of Regrets*]

The house was dark and still as a churchyard, save for the faint strains of a violin. "Where is everybody?" Aristide inquired.

"The widow's in her room, probably regaining her strength after a bout in bed with the secretary. Bouton's scraping away at his fiddle—hear it? Citizeness Bouton said she was feeling ill—she looked like death warmed over—and took off to her bed."

"Good God, you don't think—" Aristide began, but François shook his head.

"She's not poisoned, if that's what you're thinking. She's been looking like hell ever since her sister hanged herself. Let's see . . . Citizen Dupont—he's upstairs conferring with the notary about business. They've been palavering for hours. The kids are in the kitchen, helping with the crockery and scrounging food from Thérèse, last I saw."

[from *The Executioner's Heir*]

Looking back, I think I must have been a bit of a disappointment to Madame. Jacques was all right; he was four years older than I, grown up. He had some sense. But I . . . well, I was a silly teenaged kid who'd had to do without for a long time, and then suddenly found myself with fine clothes on my back and a handful of gold and silver in my pocket.

I'd grown up in the back of beyond, in that drafty château where the roof leaked, the furniture didn't match, and the moth-eaten old tapestries were in rags. So of course I thought Madame's parlor, all done up in cream and sky-blue paneling, was like a hall at Versailles. She was an aristocrat and had the income and status from her position to live like one: She gave dinner parties nearly every week and went visiting in her carriage, like a duchess. Instead of being just the two penniless whelps of the old drunk in the château, Jacques and I counted for something again; we were the cousins of the lady abbess.

Not that it was all jolly. We counted for something, but that didn't mean the town took us to their hearts straight away. Abbeville is traditional, to say the least. More like stodgy. They don't like strangers there. Everybody seems to know everybody else, and if you're a new face they'll stare at you until you start to think that maybe your nose has fallen off.

If you choose to use a slangy, modern style, however, be aware that most readers still won't let you get away—*ever*—with anachronistic *references*: in other words, with using an expression about, or referring slangily to, something that hasn't happened yet, hasn't been discovered or invented yet, or someone who hasn't been born yet. (And don't forget to hunt down and kill anachronistic references in your narration, where you, the author, are speaking; while less jarring in narrative than in characters' dialogue, they will also bring any reader who notices them to a screeching halt.)

You can't have your ancient Egyptian, no matter how casually she's speaking, describe someone as being "as flighty as a hummingbird," since hummingbirds come strictly from the Americas and no ancient Egyptian had ever heard of them (see Chapter 6, "Food, Plants, and Animals"). Nor can your Egyptian describe something disappointing or overhyped as "just a flash in the pan" two or three thousand years before the invention of small firearms. (A spark in the "pan" of a musket sometimes made only a visible but useless flare that wasn't enough to actually fire the gun; the expression came into use in English around the late 17th century, at the time of the invention of the flintlock musket.) And it's a bad idea to say in your narrative, of a Stone Age character, that "his thoughts derailed," when the railroad won't be invented for another thirty thousand years or so.

Your character or narrator can't say that two people or things are "joined like Siamese twins" before the original, famous, conjoined "Siamese Twins," Chang and Eng Bunker, born in Siam (Thailand) in 1811, became well known in the West in the 1830s. Your Tudor Englishman can't call someone a "sadist" (referring, of course, to the Marquis de Sade, who was born in 1740, while the term *sadist* wasn't coined until the mid 1800s)—even though some clueless author did put that clunker into a published novel, and an equally clueless editor let him get away with it.

Nor can your Tudor Englishman say that he's angry and "letting off steam," which literally refers to opening a valve and reducing the amount of excess steam that's running a steam engine, so that the boiler won't burst. You can't talk about a steam engine before the Industrial Revolution—and don't start arguing about how Leonardo or ancient Greek philosopher-scientists may have invented one; an invention needs to become ubiquitous before terms relating to it slip into everyday speech, and that didn't happen until well into the Industrial Revolution, say about 1800 or later to be safe.

Rewatching some of *The Tudors* not long ago, I winced to hear Cardinal Wolsey telling Sir Thomas More, after an unsuccessful diplomatic mission circa 1528, that obviously England's concerns had been "sidelined"—an expression taken from modern sports like football. And even *Downton Abbey*, despite its meticulous re-creation of early-20th-century England, has been guilty of a few dialogue howlers, now and then dropping such bombs as the trendy post-1980s expressions "parenting," "steep learning curve," and "As if!"

Ack!

There are lots of slang dictionaries out there (not to mention the Internet). There are lots of novels from all over the 19th and 20th centuries that will give you examples of slang and style of speech used in any given decade and area. Mystery novels from the "Golden Age" of classic mysteries (1880s to 1940s) will give you tons of atmosphere and authentic period dialogue (as well as endless "daily life" details) for those decades, since mysteries have to be so firmly rooted in the real life of their time to be believable.

Shakespeare will give you lots of wonderful 16th-century expressions in his lower-class characters' prose dialogue. Novels and plays from the 18th and early 19th centuries are full of marvelous and authentic period dialogue, though you'll want to "streamline" the style a bit so it doesn't sound stilted to 21st-century ears. *Use them* to get an idea of what was a common expression or style of the decade, and what was NOT, before you write another sentence. Better you should have no slang at all in your HF than make ridiculous mistakes by including slang that's half a century ahead of its time.

Original versions of clichéd expressions

For those writing HF set in English-speaking lands, a more esoteric way of getting a long-lived idiomatic expression wrong for the period is to use the modern version that we hear today: in other words, the soundalike version it's morphed into over the centuries from something a bit different.

"Dull as dishwater," for example, began its existence, some centuries ago, as the still-used-here-and-there "dull as ditchwater"; "he's the spittin' image of X" was once "he's the spit and image." (And it's entirely possible that illiterate, but vaguely plausible, modern malapropisms like the transformation of "the whole kit and caboodle" into "the whole kitten caboodle"; "a hair's breadth" into "a hare's breath"; or "nip it in the bud" to "nip it in the butt"—heaven help us!—may someday creep into common and accepted use in the same way.)

Try looking up expressions like this to see if they were slightly different back in Queen Victoria's or Shakespeare's day. Doing so, besides being more accurate, will give your dialogue a bit of additional richness and period flavor.

The whole kitten caboodle?

Two countries divided by a common language: Americanisms vs. Britishisms

During the past forty years, Americans and Brits have taken, more and more, to using each other's expressions—no doubt absorbed from imported TV shows. Until at least the middle of the 20th century, however, many words and phrases native to both Britons and Americans remained strictly on their own sides of the Atlantic and could make a conversation that was apparently in English seem incomprehensible. Some of the expressions and usages listed here may now be as familiar to transatlantic speakers as to their original users, but if you're an American writing a story set in the U.K. before 1960 or so, or vice versa, you *must* keep the differences in colloquial speech in mind.

Remember the different meanings of "pants" in American English (AmE) and British English (BrE), pointed out in the "Underpants" chapter?

American writers often incorrectly use American words or expressions when they try to write dialogue used by British characters, though "pants" (which *always* means "ladies' panties," not "trousers," to the British) is probably the funniest when it's misused in both dialogue and narrative by clueless Americans who mean "trousers." ("Sir William pulled on his pants and rushed out to the courtyard" or "During afternoon tea, Sophia covertly admired Sir William's dove-gray pants, which were a marvel of fine tailoring . . ."—Americans, substitute "panties" for "pants" and see what kind of image those sentences conjure up.)

Another common American mistake is to have British characters say "**fall**" (the season) when they should be saying "**autumn**." Actually "fall" is one of those Early Modern English words that was used in its American meaning in Shakespeare's day, traveled to the New World with the early settlers, and stayed there, while eventually disappearing in England. So you can, if you really want to, have your 16th-century Londoner say "fall" to refer to the season (although probably a lot of people will still try to correct you); but steer clear of having any British character in the 18th century or later use "fall" rather than "autumn."

Another one: Brits say "he was taken to hospital" and "he spent three days in hospital"; Americans say "he was taken to **the** hospital" and "in **the** hospital." Both Britons and Americans often get this subtle little difference wrong when putting words in the mouths of people from the other side of the pond.

Then there's the word "**sick**," which in AmE is a very general term and means "unwell" or "ill"; an American who says "I got sick last summer" can mean he came down with anything from the common cold to cancer. In modern BrE, however, at least until quite recently, "sick" specifically means "nauseous" and/or "vomiting": "he was sick" (BrE) invariably means "he vomited" ("sick to his stomach" is implied). "I feel sick" (BrE) invariably means "I feel nauseous, as if I'm about to vomit." "I felt rather sick about it" (BrE) means "It made me feel rather queasy," whether literally or figuratively.

A British character in 1850 or 1920 would never say he was "out sick with a cold yesterday," or that someone was "very sick" if she had a disease that didn't involve tossing one's cookies—she'd be *ill* with consumption, not *sick*.

And, for goodness' sake, Americans, beware of the harmless slang word "**fanny**" (meaning "backside" or "rump"), which in BrE is an *extremely* crude word for "female sexual organs," pretty much synonymous with "c**t." "Bum" (20th century and less vulgar) or "arse" (older, at least 19th century, and more vulgar) are the best British equivalents of the American "fanny" or "butt" (and the British for "fanny pack" is a "bum bag").

On a related subject, there *is* a distinct difference in BrE between the words "arse" and "ass"—an arse is a backside and only a backside, while an ass is a donkey or, by extension, a foolish or stupid or stupidly obnoxious person (and "arse" is pronounced with the British broad *a*, "ahse," to rhyme with "sparse," but "ass" is not—it always rhymes with "sass"). In Britain an upper-class twit can be a silly ass but never an arse, while a bruised bottom is a sore arse but never a sore ass, as it is in North America.

There are lots more of these wicked little language traps, though most of these differences in American and British English fortunately date from the mid 19th to early 20th centuries and often have to do with technology from those eras, when inventions sometimes developed—and were named—independently (if you're writing a story set in the 1920s, for instance, beware of all those automobile terms!). If you are an American writing about British characters, or a Briton writing about Americans, please, please get yourself a British-American phrasebook (yes, they do exist) and do try to run your manuscript past someone from the other side of the pond, to ensure that you haven't used an expression that will be unintentionally incomprehensible or hilarious to him.

Some common words and expressions used in the 19th and 20th centuries that you should always translate from American to British when Brits are speaking (and vice versa, of course):

American	British
Apartment	Flat
Apartment building	Block of flats; or less commonly "apartment block"
Bus (long-distance, intercity)	Coach (or "motor coach," early 20th century)
Closet	Cupboard
Cookie	Biscuit
Counter-clockwise	Anti-clockwise
Crazy	Mad ("mad" is rarely used to mean "angry" in BrE; while "crazy" usually describes something excessively cockeyed or crooked: "the path ran at crazy angles to the road")
Dump, garbage dump	Rubbish tip

Elevator	Lift
Flashlight	Torch
Garbage can, trash can	Dustbin, rubbish bin
Gas (gasoline)	Petrol
Hood (of a car)	Bonnet—in BrE, a car's "hood" is a convertible top
Idling (of a car)	Ticking over
In heat (sexually aroused)	On heat
Period (punctuation mark)	Full stop
Prep school	Public school—in BrE a "prep school" is a private school for pupils under 13 only
Private school	Public school
Public transportation	Public transport
Railroad	Railway
Raise (of salary)	Rise
Round trip ticket	Return ticket
Sedan (car)	Saloon
Sidewalk	Pavement
Soccer	Football
[To] stay (at a hotel, etc.)	Stop
Study, studying (for an exam)	Revise; revising; revision
Subway	Underground—in BrE, a "subway" is a pedestrian underpass
Sweater	Jumper
Truck	Lorry
Trunk (of a car)	Boot
Windshield (of a car)	Windscreen
Zero	Nought (when speaking of the typographical character 0; BrE: "There's one too many noughts in this figure.")

And be aware of these common 20th-century British slang terms that don't mean at all what an American might expect them to mean:

British	**American**
Fag	Cigarette
Fagged out	Tired out, pooped out
Hooter	Nose, especially a large one

Knock (someone) up   Wake someone up or rouse him out of bed by knocking at his door—"I'll knock you up tomorrow morning" (though the AmE meaning, "to get [someone] pregnant," seems to have taken over in recent years; the original meaning, however, persisted in BrE until at least the last decades of the 20th century)

Pissed   Drunk (but "pissed off" means the same in both BrE and AmE, though it is a recent expression; and "pissed" for "drunk" took over from "tight" sometime in the middle of the 20th century)

Readers' further suggestions for these lists will be happily accepted!

Oui, mon dieu, c'est un blague, n'est-pas? [3]

(Or, if you *must* sprinkle your novel with foreign phrases, kindly use them in such a way that a native speaker of their language would actually recognize them.)

Historical fiction is probably the only literary genre in which the majority of authors set their stories in foreign countries and/or in eras that used archaic versions of modern languages. But whether your story is set in England in 1400, Germany in 1930, or Rome in 300 B.C., if you feel you must give a few examples of the local language that your characters would actually have been speaking, you do need to get the details right.

To begin with the French (OK, semi-French) example above, *mon dieu* simply means "My God." But the French, just like speakers of English, capitalize the word "God" whenever referring to the Christian deity and it should always be written *mon Dieu*.

Blague ("joke") is a feminine noun in French, so it has to take the feminine article *une*, not the masculine *un*.

Using *n'est-pas* (meaning "isn't it?", "is that not so?") is simply grammatically *wrong*, without exception (it should be *n'est-ce pas*); the author who continually used it, and "*mon dieu*," and many other cringe-inducing examples of bad French and amateurish writing in her error-ridden "historical" novel, clearly has nothing more than a half-remembered junior-high-school grasp of French.

Use foreign phrases with a light hand. If you're writing a story set in an English-speaking country with English characters, but featuring a foreign character or two (an excellent example of this would be Agatha Christie's many mysteries featuring Belgian-born sleuth Hercule Poirot), it's customary and acceptable to put a few foreign phrases into his or her dialogue now and then, in order to remind us of the character's ethnicity—*as long as you get the phrases right*. If you

---

[3] "Yes, my God, it's a joke, isn't it?" (Sort of. If the French were correct here, which it isn't.)

don't actually speak the language well, *please* restrict your-self to a very few easy words and stock phrases. It's ex-tremely disconcerting, if the reader does speak the language which the character is presumably able to speak fluently and articulately, to come across him or her mangling it.

Remember, however, that most of your readers probably don't speak that particular language either, whatever it may be; so don't put any dialogue important to the plot in a for-eign language;[4] use it merely for color, or when the meaning is transparently clear through context, such as in these ex-amples (translations in brackets added) from Christie's *Cards On the Table*:

> *Pas si bête* [not so stupid], commented Poirot to himself. But then, no more is Hercule Poirot! If she knew me bet-ter she would realize I would never lay a *piège* [snare] as gross as that!

> "I send off my parcels very much *á l'avance* [ahead of time]," Poirot explained. ... "*Mille remerciments* [a thou-sand thanks], mademoiselle."

> "*Eh bien* [Well]," said Poirot. "The case is ended."

Probably most annoying to the reader is a story written in English—but placed entirely in a non-English-speaking setting—which is overloaded to bursting point with irrelevant snippets and words from the local language which, according to the conventions of fiction, all the characters are already speaking. Either the author is showing off the language he went to the trouble of learning just in order to research and write his novel, or else he is so desperately insecure about his writing that he needs to be sure that we always remember, while reading it, that the story is taking place in *la belle*

---

[4] As Dorothy L. Sayers did in a couple of her mysteries. Sayers spoke flu-ent French and obviously expected all her readers to do the same; it was only under extreme pressure from her editor that she added an English translation of a long letter in French that contained the entire solution to one mystery novel!

France of *le roi* Louis XIV, *oui*? Get it? 17th-century France, *n'est-ce pas*? See, I'm sticking in *beaucoup* French words so you'll always know it's France. Got it? *Oui*?

It's even more the glaring mark of a clumsy amateur if the author then manages to get the gratuitous foreign language samples wrong, like the author mentioned earlier, who liberally peppered her historical novel set entirely in 18th-century France (and featuring only French characters) with far too many throwaway, and completely unnecessary, samples of often incorrect French.

If you've written your novel properly and established your setting, we *know* your characters are 18th-century French or ancient Egyptian or medieval Japanese. We don't need to have it constantly rubbed in by seeing them say "yes" or "no" or "sweetie-pie" or "oh, darn!" in French, ancient Egyptian, or 14th-century Japanese twice in every blessed paragraph. Use your foreign language snippets *very* sparingly; readers will get it, I promise.

The only exception to this should be terms that are best left in their original language: complex words layered with meaning that would, in translation, require a whole sentence in English rather than one nice, neat, compact word in the original.

An example from my own work would be the ancient French word *bourreau*—which, today, means "executioner," but which, in the 18th century, had all kinds of negative connotations attached and which implied "brute" or "butcher" as well as the simple, neutral job description *exécuteur*, "executioner." There was a vast and important difference at the time between the words *exécuteur* and *bourreau*; I chose to give the readers the necessary explanation of *bourreau* in the course of a conversation early in the novel. I then used the word *bourreau* when required in the story, instead of choosing an inadequate English equivalent, like "hangman," which just doesn't convey the ugliness of the French word.

So if you need to use a foreign word with this kind of weighted meaning, go ahead, tell your readers what that word means early in the story, through context or a *brief* info dump or a plausible conversation between characters, or even give the readers a glossary at the beginning of the book. And then boldly go ahead and use that foreign word.

Thou must get the second person singular right, if thou'rt hell-bent upon using it

Remember the second person singular?

It's that archaic *thee-thou* form that's pretty much disappeared from modern English.

Personally, I don't recommend you use it—ever—unless you're writing about Britain in the mid 17th century or later, you have some very rustic minor characters in your story, and you'd like to emphasize just how rustic and provincial they are by having them say things like "doost 'a" ("dost thou") and "begone with 'ee" ("with thee") and "thou art." Or, of course, if you have some Quaker characters in a 17th- or 18th-century setting, and you want to emphasize their insistence on using the "familiar" form to everyone.

But if you're going to use the archaic second person singular (SPS), you'd better get it right—and use it in the right places.

The paradox with using the archaic SPS today, however, is that, since it's pretty much vanished from the English language—the only place we're likely to come across it these days is in Shakespeare or the Bible—it's so alien to us that it sounds to us like a *formal* and highfalutin' usage rather than the casual, familiar, and potentially condescending or insolent form that it actually is. "Early English translations of the Bible used *thou* and never *you* as the singular second-person pronoun," adds one linguist, "with the double effect of rescuing *thou* from complete obscurity and also imbuing it with an air of religious solemnity that is antithetical to its former sense of familiarity or disrespect."[5]

---

[5] Pressley, J. M., "Thou Pesky 'Thou'." Shakespeare Resource Centre, 8 January 2010.

One of the weirdest "super-formal" misuses of *thou*/*thee*
ever is probably in the episode "Amok Time" from the original *Star Trek* series, in which a Vulcan priestess uses "thee"
(the direct object pronoun) indiscriminately to mean "you"—
whether subject or object, singular or plural, and with the
wrong verb endings—and it's all supposed to be very formal
and ceremonial. You might make an excuse that it could be
standing in for dialogue in the Vulcan language, but honestly
it feels much more like bad pseudo-highfalutin' pseudo-archaic
grammar inflicted on us by a scriptwriter who, as is often the
case, didn't really know what he was talking about:

> T'PAU [the priestess]: And thee are called? [**incorrect**:
> thou art called]
> McCOY: Leonard McCoy, ma'am.
> T'PAU: Spock, thee names [**incorrect**: thou namest] these
> outworlders friends. How does thee [**incorrect**: dost thou]
> pledge their behavior?
> * * *
> T'PAU: It is said thy [**correct usage**] Vulcan blood is thin.
> Are thee [**incorrect**: art thou] Vulcan or are thee [**incor-
> rect**: art thou] human?
> SPOCK: I burn, T'Pau. Thee has [**incorrect**: thou hast] the
> power, T'Pau. In the name of my fathers, forbid. T'Pau, I
> plead with thee! [**correct usage**]
> T'PAU: Thee has [**incorrect**: thou hast] prided thyself [**cor-
> rect usage**] on thy [**correct usage**] Vulcan heritage. It is
> decided.

Oy!

English is alone, today, among major modern European languages in using the same pronoun ("you") to address everyone, singular or plural, deferentially or insultingly, in both
informal and formal settings. Until the mid 17th century, however, people always used "thou" as the second person singular, to address a single person with whom they were on close
terms as a friend or family member, or to address someone
socially well beneath them, such as a servant (or to insult some-

one by *implying* that s/he was socially beneath them).

"Thou"; the direct object pronoun "thee"; the possessive "thy," and the reflexive "thyself," were for rudely casual talk; talk among friendly equals; or upper class to much lower class. "You" was used only for addressing a group of two or more persons, and for politely addressing a superior, a person of higher social standing, or anyone with whom the speaker was not intimate. (In France today, for example, people use the formal "*vous*" [you] form to almost everyone except close family members and long-established best friends, with whom they use "*tu*" [thou]; and can be very much offended if someone not an intimate friend addresses them as "*tu*.")

The early Quakers, however, insisted, among other things, on equality between all members of a society, and in the 17th century this included addressing everyone, not just friends and family, as "thou," because everyone was equal before God. Most people at the time considered this practice offensive, if not downright revolutionary.

If you're writing a novel about 17th-century English Puritans and using only authentic 17th-century English speech in the dialogue (which I really don't recommend—a novel full of genuine archaic speech is an instant turnoff for most readers), your hero would address his parents, his beloved aunt, his dog, his sister, the servants, his best friend, a beggar on the street, and God (in prayer) as "thou," but would use "you" with everyone else. His Quaker cousin, on the other hand, would say "thou" to everyone, even the king, if he got the chance.

By the end of the 17th century, democratic English/American usage had eliminated the "thou" form in everyday speech and leveled the distinction between informal and formal (or superior-to-inferior) address to use the formal, polite form for everyone, no matter who they might be (even animals!). The true, archaic SPS only remains in occasional use in some isolated pockets in the British Isles, particularly Yorkshire and Scotland, where regional dialects are still strong.

But if you *must* use the archaic SPS, let's use the grammar properly:

Some common irregular verbs:

"To be":

>Second person plural (& modern second person singular): You are

>Archaic second person singular: **Thou art** (but usually "thou'rt" in casual speech)

"To have":

>Second person plural (& modern second person singular): You have

>Archaic second person singular: **Thou hast** (sometimes "thou'st" in casual speech)

(To be able to) "can," "may"; (to have to) "must":

>Second person plural (& modern second person singular): You can

>Archaic second person singular: **Thou canst**

>Second person plural (& modern second person singular): You may

>Archaic second person singular: **Thou mayest** or **mayst** (usually pronounced "mayst")

>**BUT: Thou must** (**not** the *extremely* archaic "thou must-est" unless you're getting Early Medieval with your readers)

"To do":

>Second person plural (& modern second person singular): You do

>Archaic second person singular: **Thou doest** or **dost**

"Will"

> Second person plural (& modern second person singular): You will

> Archaic second person singular: **Thou wilt**

And a few regular verbs:

"To like":

> Second person plural (& modern second person singular): You like

> Archaic second person singular: **Thou likest**

"To bring":

> Second person plural (& modern second person singular): You bring

> Archaic second person singular: **Thou bringest**

"To eat":

> Second person plural (& modern second person singular): You eat

> Archaic second person singular: **Thou eatest**

"To ride":

> Second person plural (& modern second person singular): You ride
> Archaic second person singular: **Thou ridest**

You get the idea by now, I'm sure. Just add "est" (or "st" if the verb infinitive ends in *e*) to the end of a regular verb and you've got your SPS form.

The direct object pronoun, *Thee*, and the possessive pronoun, *Thy*

Thee gets mangled all the time, usually by being used as the subject pronoun (see the *Star Trek* example above), just as the direct object pronouns "him/her" are often misused as subject pronouns "s/he" in contemporary speech. (Wrong: "Anne and him went to the park." Right: "He and Anne went to the park." Wrong: "Her and I liked the movie." Right: "She and I liked the movie." **Wrong: "Thee must go now." Right: "Thou must go now."**) *Thee* is used as **the object of the sentence**—the one to or against whom an action is directed—and at no other time: "I'll wait for thee." "I do not think she likes thee." "Did he hit thee hard?"

Throw in the possessive pronoun, **thy**, and the reflexive **thyself**: "Did thy [poss] horse throw thee [dir obj]? Didst thou [subj] hurt thyself [reflexive]? Let me look at thy [poss] arm."

Once again, it's probably better to avoid the SPS in the first place. But if you just have to use it, these basic guidelines should keep you on the right track.

5

Anachronisms Of Attitude: Misplaced Political Correctness & Feisty Females

"Learn to tolerate strange world views. Don't pervert the values of the past. Women in former eras were downtrodden and frequently assented to it. Generally speaking, our ancestors were not tolerant, liberal or democratic. Your characters probably did not read [the liberal newspaper] *The Guardian*, and very likely believed in hellfire, beating children and hanging malefactors. Can you live with that?"

Hilary Mantel, on writing historical fiction

any authors of "historical" fiction are guilty of a fault that a professor of literature or history would call "presentism." For our purposes, that's an inability on the part of the author to tear his mindset away from the familiar aspects of his own lifetime—like the author mentioned previously who, no matter how carefully she described the look, atmosphere, and technology of wartime London, continually put 1990s American expressions in the mouths, and socially liberal 21st-century opinions in the minds, of her 1940s British characters.

An author guilty of presentism may think she's telling us all about the Florence of the Medici when meticulously describing the clothes, the food, and the horse manure on the cobblestoned streets, but if characters start talking earnestly about human rights and religious tolerance and isn't it a shame that we don't have those, she's still providing anachronistic 21st-century mindsets to go with her 16th-century trappings. In short, presentism is the conscious or unconscious assumption (there's that horrible word *assume* again!) that, especially in intangibles like speech and attitudes, people in the past were no different from those in the present.

Anachronistic attitudes in HF can be even sneakier and harder to spot and demolish than anachronistic objects and speech. One of the most common complaints among voracious readers of HF is "cosplay," which, in fan communities, means dressing up in historical or fantasy outfits (while, no doubt, keeping your cell phone handy at your sword belt), but in HF means—unfortunately—that the characters in an unsatisfying novel are merely "modern people in costumes."

When a character in a novel set 400 years ago, for instance, starts to loudly declare his or her enlightened views about slavery (it's wrong!) or women's rights (they're good!) or religious tolerance (it should exist for everyone, including unbelievers!) or some other issue that most of us, in the 21st-century Western world, do take for granted, but which were not even considered in 1600, such a blatantly presentist attitude can rip us right out of the story. The same goes for a 1600 character who blithely ignores the intense religious influence and religious controversy that pervades his or her world. The area's and period's religion and all its customs and strictures never seem to make a whit of difference to the character's life or actions; the strongly religious aspect of life in almost any past century, including the highly industrialized and technological 19th century, can pretty much slide past an author who isn't a churchgoer herself. And when a character blithely ignores the fact that hereditary absolute (more or less) monarchies were so firmly established in western Europe in 1600 that no one would waste a moment considering an alternative, and earnestly announces that the ancient Romans had it right and France or Spain or England would be better as a democracy, because democracy was a much better idea than monarchy . . . well, coming across any of these attitudes can be just as jarring as reading about Henry VIII eating a peanut butter sandwich.

Some authors, especially of formula romances (or formula histo-mysteries featuring plucky female amateur crime-solvers from all eras), just don't grasp the Taliban-worthy social limitations imposed on high-caste European or American women at almost any time before, say, World War I. When, in a historical novel not set on the frontier and taking place before 1915 or so, a spunky young unmarried woman from an upper-class family sneaks off unaccompanied to meet a lover or solve a mystery, readers' eyebrows ought to go up. When the spunky young unmarried woman sneaks off alone in a large city where anything could happen, and never worries about her sheer physical safety in the inevitable scary area where unaccompanied women are considered fair game for thieves and rapists, this bears no relationship whatsoever to reality. And when no one responsible for the spunky young unmarried woman makes a peep of protest or outrage at her disgraceful behavior, or suggests that her reputation and marriageability may now be severely compromised, the whole situation becomes even more ludicrous. Read up on modern Saudi Arabian society and its intense religiosity, sexual prudery, and severe limitations placed on all women, when you try to imagine how restrictive and narrow young, upper-class, unmarried Western women's lives could have been in past centuries—even in notoriously uninhibited eras like the 17th or 18th centuries in western Europe, when *married* adults tended to revel in promiscuity.

As a fan of history, you may remember that in the year 2000, during the first wave of popularity of "reality shows," a British TV production company decided to ride the wave and produce one—but a classy, pop-intellectual reality show, of course, suitable for PBS viewers in the USA. This was a program called *The 1900 House* and it took a "typical" English middle-class family of 2000 (father, mother, four children), put them in period clothing, and plunked them down for three months into a late-19th-century, modest-middle-class London house, which had been stripped of all its 20th-century improvements and refitted with only fixtures, furnishings, equipment, products, and provisions that it would have had in the year 1900 (plus TV cameras, of course, including one that the family could gripe to directly about discomfort and inconvenience). Actors in 1900 costume appeared at the door as greengrocers and butchers delivering the day's groceries. The family was allowed to go out only to venues dating from the late Victorian period that had been redecorated to resemble their 1900 past. And the mother was given a strict weekly budget in 1900 currency and prices.

Interesting experiment.

But.

First of all, for some reason, they chose a family in which the mother was a vegetarian and insisted on remaining one throughout the show. Nothing wrong with that—except that vegetarians were far, far, *far* less common in 1900 London than in 2000 London. In 1900, 99.9% of everybody ate lots of "flesh" as a matter of course. Middle-class British dinners in 1900 were as meat- and starch-heavy and unimaginative ("Boiled Everything," anyone?) as middle-class American dinners in 1940, if not more so. If you were too poor to afford meat very often, you ate fried fish (hence the enduring popularity of fish and chips—it was the cheap and ubiquitous food of the working classes for decades). In the 19th century, only socialistic, bohemian, slightly wacky artistic, literary, or intellectual types like George Bernard Shaw were vegetarians— the expression "health nut" hadn't been invented yet, but if it had, people would have used it to describe someone who refused to eat meat, with a strong emphasis on the "nut" part.

If the production company wanted to feature a family that would have even a chance of fitting in to its 1900 environment, why begin by deliberately including someone (a member of a smallish minority of British citizens even in the year 2000) who would have an immediate, obvious, highly anachronistic, difficult issue with something that had been a major and, essentially, non-negotiable part of everyday life in 1900? No doubt it was to introduce an added bit of conflict and inconvenience into the show to spice it up, but many history fan viewers found it merely annoying.

The mother in the show was definitely an example of somebody who was much too 21st-century-P.C. to cope with a typical 1900 lifestyle. After a few weeks of trying to cook and clean for a household of six people, using 1900 tools and supplies and sticking to typical 1900 menus and standards of hygiene, she finally gave in and hired a maid of all work (an actress) to help out. Any middle-class family of 1900 would have had at least one servant, and Elizabeth, the maid, as a typical young, uneducated, relatively unskilled servant girl of 1900 London, was expected to take over the worst, dirtiest, dullest, hardest jobs, for her room and board plus laughably low pay. After a few weeks of this, however, the mother, though she could afford Elizabeth's pay and board out of her housekeeping budget, felt so uncomfortable about "exploiting" a servant, particularly a female servant, for such work that she dismissed the girl.

These two examples point out the essential problem of fitting a square peg (modern family) into a round hole (1900 surroundings). You can give modern flesh-and-blood people period atmosphere and period dress and period surroundings, but

you're still dealing with presentism: you can't give them the appropriate period attitudes.

While the mother in *The 1900 House* refused to eat meat, and felt guilty about hiring a servant girl because she felt she was "taking unfair advantage" of a fellow female (chafing at her circa-1900 restrictions, she'd inevitably become interested in the suffragette movement, the closest thing to women's liberation at the time), no one in 1900 would have thought twice about either issue. A middle-class housewife in 1900 who felt she was taking unfair advantage of a young woman by hiring her to do the dirty work would be like somebody today feeling guilty about taking advantage of a vacuum cleaner. (See more about this in Chapter 14, "Servants.")

It never seemed to have occurred to the mother that, rather than "oppressing" her 1900 maidservant, a 1900 housewife would have been giving a desperately poor young girl from the London slums a badly needed and scarce job and place to live (not to mention three meals a day), no matter how hard the work. Moreover, subsequently letting her go was scarcely "liberating" a servant from an unpleasant job so that she could find a better one—in 1900 there *weren't* significantly better jobs than domestic service available for girls of her class and training. Think of *Pygmalion* (1912): Eliza Doolittle, the flower girl from the back streets, wants to learn how to speak with a "posh" accent so that she can get a job in a flower shop rather than just sell flowers out of a basket on the sidewalk. In 1912, even a relatively bottom-of-the-heap job like counter girl in a luxury shop wasn't available to a young woman from the slums with a working-class accent, working-class manners, and minimal education.

The sole alternatives to domestic service, for girls like Elizabeth, were equally exhausting, low-paying, often much more dangerous, unskilled factory jobs, such as in match factories, where the mostly female workers often developed phosphorus poisoning; or in cloth mills with heavy machinery in which workers might easily lose fingers, hands, or even their lives in accidents. Or, of course, there was prostitution—if you were beautiful and lucky, in a red-velvet Victorian bordello, but more likely in back alleys in the slums. In short, dismissing a servant who had no other skills wasn't doing her a favor; it was, rather, thrusting her on the streets once again to fend for herself amid high unemployment and squalid home conditions.

This, while not HF, is a good, real-life example of a modern "politically correct" mindset that simply wouldn't have existed before the late 20th century—in this case, feeling somehow elitist and/or exploitative by doing something (hiring a servant) that anyone in a previous century would have done in the blink of an eye and never felt the least whiff of guilt about. And although we don't want to allow bigoted or offensive statements to creep into our work, it's far too easy to let an overt and heavy-handed display of presentism and political correctness to creep in instead, which can make a work of HF ludicrous.

Women, for instance, for most of Western history, have been viewed by most men as slightly subhuman cook-housekeepers and providers of sexual gratification (and, inevitably, baby-making machines)—created by whatever god they worship not as partners in a marriage, but as little more than servants to the breadwinning male, and creatures to be ignored whenever the man felt like it, rather like a useful but annoying dog that could be tied up outside when it barked or begged too much. (Don't jump all over me. There are plenty of exceptions: but let's agree that at least 80% of men, particularly uneducated peasant and working-class men, for the past few thousand years in most Western cultures—Europe, the ancient Mediterranean, and European America—have considered their women-folk so, at least until well into the 20th century. Watch *All in the Family* from the early 1970s for a comic portrait of a conservative, middle-aged, minimally educated blue-collar American couple that Women's Lib passed by at a long, long distance. And many parts of the world still haven't caught up.)

The Western ideas of feminism and women's rights, meanwhile—even the idea that women, on the whole, were intellectually equal to men—were just beginning to stir toward the end of the 18th century and picked up steam around the middle of the 19th. So putting a strident, defiant, independent-minded feminist, no matter how aristocratic, intelligent, well-educated, and shrewd she may be, who believes and declares that all women should be equal to men in all things and should be allowed to do anything men do and should *never ever* have their marriages arranged for them—and who isn't promptly regarded as a lunatic or a witch—into a novel set in 200 B.C. or A.D. 1200 or even A.D. 1700 immediately makes the story as ridiculous as the improbable plots of some "historical" romances.

This isn't to say that all women in male-dominated societies throughout history were subservient, subjugated, and dependent. Far from it. Plenty of women were earning their own living—those from poor families had to or starve—and only left their jobs when they married, after which housekeeping, child-rearing, and possibly a paid-by-the-piece job such as spinning thread or weaving, which a woman could do at home when she had a spare moment, would take up all their time and energy. Plenty of widows owned and ran their own small businesses—some inherited from their husbands, others created with their own initiative; most medieval noblewomen routinely managed their husbands' estates when the men were off at war. We all know about Joan of Arc and Boadicea, and the brilliant and politically savvy queens and empresses who did a much better job ruling their kingdoms than did many of their male predecessors (though a few utter failures, such as Mary Stuart, may come to mind as well).

But working, warring, or ruling women of the past, while they knew they were quite as capable as men of getting the job done, weren't agitating for women's rights in a world where the idea hadn't been born yet, and loudly protesting that the male chauvinists were oppressing them. (Which, by the way, is a Women's Movement expression of the mid 20th century, and even the broad term "chauvinist"—one who aggressively promotes a specific idea or group as superior to all other alternatives—dates from no earlier than the Napoleonic Wars: so, for heaven's sake, don't use the phrase "male chauvinist"—ever—unless your novel is set in the 1960s or later!)

Even Elizabeth I, one of the strongest and most successful women in history, who knew how to captivate powerful men and manipulate the male-dominated system to her benefit, didn't have "liberate English women and decree gender equality" on her to-do list. Aside from being determined to stay in power herself and not share any portion of her power with a foreign husband, she wasn't exactly a 16th-century version of a militant feminist.

Smart women simply worked with what they had, in order to achieve their goals.

So here you have the challenge of creating realistic yet appealing female characters in a historical novel for a 21st-century audience. Modern readers of fiction, two-thirds of whom are female, don't want to read about passive, languishing women (like Kitty above, gazing adoringly at big strong Tom), even when said women exist in a thoroughly male-dominated society. A sappy or passive or downtrodden female character may be all right in a supporting role, but modern Western attitudes simply don't allow readers to identify any more with fragile, drippy, utterly sweet heroines—helpless princesses always in need of rescue. (Is there any living fan of *A Tale of Two Cities*, for instance, who isn't irritated by domestic goddess Lucie Manette's eternal, bland, passive perfection? The most vigorous attribute you can apply to her is that she has "quiet strength"—though she never *does* anything much with it except bear up and be lovingly encouraging to her menfolk—father, husband, devoted secret admirer—who are taking all the active roles. Yet she was obviously Dickens's—and many other Victorian readers'—ideal woman.)

Psychologists will tell us that essential human nature and behavior—as opposed to cultural mindsets—haven't changed much over the millennia. So probably the same proportion of smart, strong human beings to dull-witted, submissive human beings (of both sexes) existed three hundred years ago, or three thousand years ago, as exists today. The challenge for the historical author is to create a fictional woman who has the same appealing intelligence and strength of character as the heroine of a 21st-century contemporary novel—a woman who's had far more opportunities to choose her own way in life and career—*without* giving the historical woman a presentist, unrealistic, overly independent or defiant or ahead-of-her-time or stridently politically correct or (ugh) "feisty" 21st-century mindset.

The realistic historical female character may very well be smarter and braver than most of the men around her—but she doesn't, unless she is the heroine of a 1970s bodice-ripper, get fed up with the empty-headed frivolities of her womanly role and run away from her aristocratic home to become a cross-dressing highwayman (er, -*person*); rather, she uses her brains and courage to work within the confines of her world, and the boundaries that the male-dominated society has set, to achieve her ends. (My own cross-dressing character in my mystery *Game of Patience*, set in 1796 Paris—a character loosely based on a real woman of the time—after a series of harsh experiences that have driven her to some extremes of behavior, has gone far, far beyond the accepted boundaries and knows it, and is beyond caring—she knows there will be no happy bodice-ripper ending. And there isn't.)

Read *I, Claudius*, one of the best historical novels ever written, and you'll pretty quickly get the idea that Livia, wife of Emperor Augustus and mother of Tiberius, as portrayed by Robert Graves, was the *real* emperor of Rome (whatever the facts about the historical Livia, a highly intelligent and ambitious daughter of an aristocratic family, may actually have been). Did the fictional Livia stride around the Forum, defiantly trumpeting ideas of female equality and how women ought to have the right to take part in the republican government, or throw on a toga and a false beard and join the army or the Senate, in order to get the power she craved?

Not on your life. In first-century B.C. Roman society, such actions would have made her something between a laughingstock and a criminal.

Fictional Livia knew that, in her patriarchal Roman society, her path to power was in marrying, and then manipulating, the right men. She was beautiful enough to attract any man she'd set her sights on, and smart enough to predict which would be the winning side in the civil wars (the intelligent and calculating Gaius Octavius, future Emperor Augustus, rather than the charismatic but self-indulgent party-boy Mark Antony): She divorced her current husband and married Octavius. Then she simply dominated him, and the rest of her menfolk, by the force of her personality and intelligence; manipulated or duped anyone, male or female, who could be useful to her; and quietly poisoned anybody important who refused to be dominated or manipulated and who got in her way. (We really don't like her much—but we have to have a sneaking admiration for her.) No ancient Roman women's lib here; but the novel gives us a convincing portrayal of a woman, via the strong influence she had on her husband and son, who was essentially running the whole show for decades . . . even though Augustus always thinks *he* is in control of the empire.

Scarlett O'Hara, for another example, is forever doing "unsuitable" things in order to get what she wants. But her inappropriate actions are frowned upon not because *no* woman of her time would have done them, but because they are not ladylike: They are things that her society decrees a genteel 1860s Southern belle of the wealthy plantation-owning class should not have been doing.

In order to achieve her goals—which range from breaking free of the dreary strictures of mid-Victorian Southern widowhood in order not to be bored out of her mind, to getting the man she loves, to sheer physical survival—Scarlett does defy the conventions of her highly conservative, upper-class, male-dominated upbringing. She often behaves, to the despair of her mother, her disapproving mammy, and the neighbors, like a woman of a far less genteel and sheltered class (or even like a brash Yankee woman—horrors!)—*but she never anachronistically pushes her way into a domain where women are unknown.*

When Scarlett takes over the running of ineffectual husband Frank's general store, and then goes into business for herself as the owner-manager of a sawmill, people disapprove not because she is going into business, which many women, especially the war widows, did, but because "ladies" of good family weren't supposed to go into such aggressive lines of business. *Particularly* not when they had husbands around who ought to have been doing it for them while the ladies stayed respectably at home and poured tea.

But Scarlett, aside from a few fairly understandable and universal "*Oh, I wish I were a man, then I'd . . .*" moments, never anachronistically pines for or demands the exceptional freedom and gender equality that most 21st-century American women now have. She doesn't even yearn for the degree of women's liberation—such as voting rights, or social freedom for unmarried young women—that had been achieved at the time of the writing of *Gone With the Wind* (late 1920s), even though she is one of the spunkiest, toughest female characters in historical fiction. And, it must be noted, she doesn't get away scot-free with flouting conventions and ignoring the neighbors' disapproval, as so many heroines of category romances seem to—her respectable social circle frowns, whispers, criticizes her, and at last nearly snubs her altogether for her behavior until Rhett Butler realizes that their daughter's social future is being jeopardized by Scarlett's brazen and un-seemly conduct, and takes steps to ingratiate himself with the "old cats."

By the way, when you're describing your spunky, spiri-ted, strong-willed, outspoken, and indomitable heroine, you

might want to choose another adjective than the vastly over-used (and really annoying, at this point) word "feisty" unless it's North America in the 1890s or later, which is when the word first seems to have appeared beyond very spotty occasional usage here and there in the Ame-rican South. And you might al-so want to know that the word originally was used to describe a small, bad-tempered dog, usu-ally a smelly one, and it de-rived from the Old German/ Old English word *fisting*, "break-ing wind"—better known as "farting"!

Basic Rules
You Need To Keep In Mind
That Will Help You Avoid
the Silly Mistakes

General Rule
No. 2

Wikipedia is Your Friend

es, I know that junior high school teachers are always telling kids not to go to Wikipedia to do their research for their school report on Abraham Lincoln, because any joker or idiot or beyond-the-fringe nutcase can insert something completely inaccurate on almost any page and make it look like a hard fact. And they're right; you probably shouldn't rely much, if at all, on Wikipedia if you need in-depth information about a real person or a major event in history, particularly controversial ones—practical jokers and monomaniacs and Wikipedia trolls love to alter pages to suit themselves.

For your important research, stick to print. Go to the library or the bookstore and the professionally published books, where a professional editor with a certain amount of knowledge and education has tried to make sure that there aren't too many mistakes or biased opinions in the history—and nobody can mess with the facts in a paper book afterward.

On the other hand, Wikipedia and the Internet in general are invaluable for a quick look at the tons of minor background information and little "everyday life" factual details you'll need for your historical novel (*never assume!*)—such as when Europeans began to drink coffee (mid 1600s) or if an ancient Roman could have ever seen a tulip (only if he'd been to the mountains of Persia) or if Napoleon might have eaten mashed potatoes (potatoes, yes; mashed, no). (Internet trolls and people with an axe to grind, for instance, probably aren't going to amuse themselves inserting incorrect information or obnoxious jokes on a Wikipedia page about non-controversial subjects like vegetables. Not when there are so many politicians and "reality TV" stars that they can insult and poke fun at instead.)

You can be 99.9% sure that the Wikipedia page about, say, dandelions is accurate. So for goodness' sake take two minutes to look up dandelions there, and elsewhere on the Internet, and learn that they originated in Eurasia, and that they were (unfortunately for lawn owners everywhere) brought to the Americas as a food plant by European settlers; and that, therefore, you should NOT describe dandelions dotting the grass in your novel about the Lakota in the year 1400 or the Pilgrims landing in the *Mayflower* in 1620. You can be 99.9% sure that the Wikipedia page about a minor historical figure who'll appear briefly in the background of your novel at least gets the dates of his birth and death correct, if all you really needed to know was his age in 1239.

Say it again: *Wikipedia is your friend.*

If you are not 100% positive that a minor thing, person, event, place, food, animal, custom, book, song—*anything*—could have appeared in your novel as you're saying it does, *look it up.*

Even if you *are* 100% positive about that minor detail, look it up anyway.

I "knew" that the Montansier Theater was a real theater in late-18th-century Paris (correct), and that it was around in Paris during the French Revolution (correct), and had been around in the 1780s as well (not quite correct!) and so didn't check my trivial, throwaway facts before the book went into print. And that's how that casual reference to the Montansier Theater of 1786, which wasn't established in Paris until 1790, got into my novel.

With Wikipedia and the rest of the Internet available at

his fingertips, an author no longer has any excuse for the silly mistakes he makes because he *assumes* that dandelions have always been annoying Americans, and so happily describes meadows full of bright yellow dandelions growing wild all over the future Massachusetts Bay Colony in his novel about the Pilgrims landing.

All together now: *Never assume.*

Go turn on your Internet browser and *look it up*.

6

Anachronisms: Food, Plants, & Animals

his chapter includes the great big grand-daddy of anachronisms in HF—feeding characters foods they couldn't possibly have been able to eat at their period of history or their location on the globe. There are so many, many ways to unwittingly insert anachronisms into your HF, but this is the most common one by far, and mostly for one reason:

The New World and the Old World

The first thing the author of any historical fiction set before 1700 or so has to keep in mind, when mentioning what the novel's hero is wearing or eating for dinner, is one word and one date:

COLUMBUS
1492

That's Christopher Columbus, the guy who discovered the Americas. Remember him?

We won't get into an argument about who actually "discovered" America first. The Vikings certainly got there 500 years before Columbus did and left traces of their settlement behind them in Newfoundland, Canada. Probably some Stone Age Europeans got there ten or twenty thousand years ago, as well as the Stone Age Siberians who were the ancestors of our present Native Americans. Probably a few Japanese or Dark Ages Celts or Knights Templar got there at some point.

But none of them made it back home to Europe or Asia and publicized the fact so that the word got out to the rest of Europe or Asia.

While Christopher Columbus, we can all agree, was the one who landed in the New World in October of 1492, did some exploring, and then got the word out to Spain, which then spread to the rest of the Old World, that there was this big land mass, sitting on the other side of the globe in the area where he'd expected China and India to be, that nobody among the Powers That Be seemed to know about.

"1492" is the first thing you need to tattoo on your arm when you're dealing with historical foodstuffs, because the number of foods and plants (and occasionally animals) of New World origin that hilariously turn up in insufficiently researched stories set in the ancient world and the Middle Ages can boggle the mind.

The author, for example, who has done minimal and sloppy research knows that the Irish eat a lot of potatoes, and have eaten a lot of potatoes for a long time, and *assumes . . .* you get my drift. So he thinks he's being terribly clever by mentioning that his seventh-century Irish Gaelic hero had a good meal of potatoes and roast meat. Well, that would be nice, except for one little fact: Potatoes originally came from South America, high up in the Andes. No Irishman—no European anywhere—had ever *heard* of a potato until the 1500s at the earliest. But because the author didn't take a minute and a half to look up *Potatoes, origins of*, in Wikipedia, you get a Dark Ages Irishman eating food that no one in Ireland would eat for another thousand years.

New World foods have become such a part of many Old World cultures' classic cuisines that it's hard to imagine such fare without them. Italian food without tomatoes? An Irish or Central European meal without potatoes? West African stews without peanuts? Indian curries without chilies—or, for that matter, potatoes and tomatoes?

(And life anywhere without *chocolate*???)

But it's a fact, Jack, that none of these cuisines had access to these now-essential ingredients before the 1500s-1600s.

So, first of all, you need to know by heart the list of foods, plants, plant products, and animals that originated in the Americas and could not possibly have been eaten or used *or referred to in any way* by anyone in Europe, Asia, or Africa before the 16th century:

- Avocados

- Beans[6]

- Chilies and green/red/yellow "peppers"[7]

- Chipmunks

- Cocoa and chocolate

- Corn (maize, sweetcorn)

- Guinea pigs

- Hummingbirds

- Llamas

- Peanuts

---

[6] Green "string" beans and many common dry varieties like navy beans, kidney beans, pinto beans, etc.—though not soybeans, chickpeas, fava beans, brown/green lentils, red lentils, mung beans, or green/yellow peas, all of which are Eurasian. All those fancy-sounding beans with Italian names, such as cannellini, borlotti, and even "Roman," are varieties bred during the past 500 years from imported New World stock.

[7] Any variation from tiny super-hot Thai chilies to serranos to poblanos to jalapeños to sweet bell peppers [capsicums].

- Poison ivy/poison oak
  - Potatoes
  - Rubber
  - Skunks
  - Squash[8]
  - Sunflowers
- Sweet potatoes
  - Tobacco
  - Tomatoes
  - Turkeys
  - Vanilla

These are just the most common items. There are many more. Look up the "Columbian Exchange" or the individual food/plant/animal you're mentioning, to be sure that you're not putting South American foods on the tables of ancient Romans or the trenchers of medieval Englishmen—or having your medieval Englishman call someone who's done him a bad turn a "dirty skunk."

Look it up. Every time.

The even trickier part of this stuff is knowing when a specific non-native food or plant or animal actually became well known and widespread in a certain area. You can be dead certain, for instance, if you've dutifully looked up potatoes, that no European would be eating them in 1490. But if you have all of your Irish characters living on them in 1500 or even 1590, you'd still be wrong—even though it's a century after Columbus. Why? Because commodities take a while to be introduced into new regions—especially when travel is

---

[8] Of all kinds, soft- and hard-shelled, winter and summer, from zucchini [courgettes] to pumpkins—though not inedible hard-shelled gourds, which are Eurasian and are members of the cucumber family.

slow and difficult—and take even longer, in some cases, for people to become willing to try them. Highly perishable foods, meanwhile, that have to grow in certain regions (like the tropics), are dependent on how long it takes to ship them to wherever you want them to end up, and if your shipping relies on the wind and takes months, forget it—your foodstuff probably was almost unknown in other continents until the late 19th century.

The Spanish, the first European conquerors and colonizers of the New World, were also the first to bring back New World foods to Europe (and soon to Asia, where there were many small outposts of Spanish traders and Catholic missionaries by the 1500s). Our old friend the potato was introduced to Europe and Asia by the Spanish, who quickly made potatoes, tomatoes, sweet bell peppers, and very mild chilies a significant part of their own cuisine—they remain so to this day. But the potato took another century to reach the British Isles; it was probably introduced by Sir Walter Raleigh (late 1500s). Peasants in Ireland, however, still weren't making potatoes the mainstay of their diet until the mid 1600s.

Though the fried potato was an exotic delicacy for Louis XIV and his court (late 1600s), French peasants weren't regularly eating potatoes until the late 1700s, and then only because a scholarly doctor named Parmentier had made it his mission to acquaint the suspicious peasantry, who preferred to stick with wheat, with the virtues, cheapness, and ease of cultivation of the mysterious tuber. Most white North Americans and many Europeans wouldn't touch tomatoes until the early 1800s (or even later—the 1920s in some remote parts of France[9]), because they thought they were poisonous—a not altogether irrational belief, since tomatoes belong to the same plant family as deadly nightshade, and eating tomato *leaves*, as every backyard vegetable gardener should know, won't do you any good at all.

Bananas, to use another example (though they're native

---

[9] Discussed in William Wiser, *The Twilight Years: France in the 1930s.*

to southeast Asia, not the Americas), weren't really known in Europe until as late as the last decades of the 19th century, because they need a tropical climate to grow and they don't travel nearly as well as oranges and other relatively sturdy fruits that are native to warm climates. Until fast, reliable steamships appeared in the later 1800s, your load of bananas from the Caribbean would probably have arrived in England, after six or eight weeks aboard a sailing ship, as tons of moldy black goo. (We won't even talk about travel from Asia, which would—before 1870 and the Suez Canal—involve another two or three months of sailing around Africa.)

Decorative plants, not being "useful" as a cheap or delicious source of food, took even longer to spread from their areas and continents of origin. Before you put a forsythia bush in an 18th-century American garden, as my grandmother did in one of her Revolutionary War children's books set in western Massachusetts (where she lived, undoubtedly with lots of forsythia in the yard), *look it up.* And you'll discover that forsythia is native to Asia and it was still very rare in the British Isles by the middle of the 19th century, so it wasn't growing all over New England in 1774.

New World animals (with one exception) were extremely unlikely to be found, except perhaps as occasional curiosities, in the Old World before the 20th century. The Americas have almost no native animals, unlike Eurasia, that are both easily domesticated and worth domesticating for their meat, their hair or skins, or their size and strength—the notable exception being the turkey, which was raised for food by the Aztecs. (The domestic chicken, the sheep, the horse, the pig, the goat, the cow, the camel, the water buffalo, etc, all originated in Eurasia.)

The only large native domesticated beast of burden in the Americas before the arrival of the Spanish was the llama, and its cousins the guanaco and alpaca, which were raised for meat, wool, and as pack animals. But no member of the llama family is big and strong enough to be ridden by an adult human or to pull wagons or plows—and so Europeans, with horses, sheep, and cattle of their own, had no need for them and did not export them to Europe except as exotic zoo animals.[10] Turkeys, however, did go back with the conquistadors and soon were raised for food and became a delicacy in Europe in subsequent centuries.

Wild animals from the Americas, moreover, have no place running wild in your story if it's set in the Old World. The American author who—probably *assuming* that what she could see in her own back yard would also be elsewhere—put a family of cute chipmunks (a strictly North American rodent) on the lawn of an estate in Kent, England in 1810, needed to do a little more homework.

In short: *never assume.* Look it up. Every time. If you're writing a story set in England in 1600, unless you manage to remember that Shakespeare mentions a handkerchief "spotted with strawberries" in *Othello*, go make sure that the English

---

[10] A llama or alpaca, along with a freak four-horned goat, both undoubtedly relics of someone's private zoo, are among the various creepily preserved 18th-century animal (and human) cadavers displayed in the museum of Paris's 250-year-old veterinary college—featured in my novel *The Cavalier of the Apocalypse* and which can be visited today. http://musee.vet-alfort.fr/

had strawberries in 1600. The next time it might be grape-fruit—and the English sure didn't have grapefruit (which are an 18th-century tropical hybrid from Jamaica) in 1600. Five minutes' worth of research on the Internet will tell you if the food or animal you're thinking of could possibly have been on your heroine's dinner plate or estate.

Aside: What's with "corn" in the Middle Ages and so on, anyway? If corn comes from the Americas, then what's it doing in medieval England?

It isn't. The trouble with the word "corn" is that, until quite recently, the word meant one thing to Americans and some-thing completely different to Britons.

The word "corn" has been around in English for a long, long time, but in the British Isles, from the Middle Ages right through the 19th century, "corn" wasn't a specific foodstuff but a general term for nearly any domesticated grain plant— usually the most commonly grown grain in a region—and of-ten was understood to mean "wheat."

> "A beautiful landscape, with the corn bright in it, but not abundant. Patches of poor rye where corn should have been, patches of poor peas and beans, patches of most coarse vegetable substitutes for wheat."
>
> [*A Tale of Two Cities* (1859)]

Here Dickens uses "corn" to mean "wheat." If an Eliza-bethan poet or Victorian novelist mentions "a golden field of corn" or "corn-colored hair," you can be absolutely sure that he's speaking of "wheat" or "grain" and not the yellow (or red or blue) stuff that grows on cobs, from which we make polenta, taco shells, and Cheez Puffs. Even today, you're more likely to be understood in the U.K., when talking about the yellow stuff that grows on cobs, if you call it "maize" or "sweetcorn."

Early English settlers in the northeastern American colo-nies, however, were hugely dependent on the local, plentiful native grain, maize, the yellow stuff that grows on cobs, which the Native Americans showed them how to cultivate. The first English colonists, having never seen it before, naturally called it "Indian corn"—Indian grain—to distinguish it from their own European "corn" (wheat, barley, oats, and/or rye) that they had brought with them across the Atlantic and which hadn't grown very well in "the New England," and the name stuck. Eventually the "Indian" part was dropped in ordinary American usage and modern Americans use the word "corn" to mean one plant and grain only. (Though we still say "Indian corn" to refer to the dried, multicolored, barely edible ears that decorate doors and tables around Thanksgiving, the original expression has lingered on in just one actual food item, which you might find at a specialty bakery: the "rye and Injun loaf," a type of bread—the basic recipe dating from at least the early 1700s—made of rye flour and, you guessed it, cornmeal.)

And do I really have to mention tobacco and smoking?

Well, obviously I do, since the unfortunate amateur writer mentioned in the introduction gave her 11th-century knight a cigar. Oh, dear, oh, dear . . . **Tobacco, just like the potato, the tomato, and corn on the cob, comes from the Americas and no European had ever heard of it before the early 1500s**. Columbus is usually credited with bringing tobacco to Europe, and the legend goes that Sir Walter Raleigh introduced the leaf, and the odd custom of the American "savages" of breathing its smoke during rituals, to England in the 1590s. (While many cultures have smoked many different plant products throughout history, the practice seems to have died out in Europe by the Dark Ages, because smoking the New World leaf began as an entirely novel concept.)

Examples of Europeans puffing on pipes (and, heaven help us, cigars!) have turned up more often than once in published stories set well before the discovery of the Americas—most painfully, perhaps, in a novel featuring the "Little Princes in the Tower" (that's 1483-85), in which the two princes' mean jailer bullies them by puffing pipe smoke in their faces . . . seven years before Columbus reached the New World and more than a century before any Englishman entertained the bizarre idea of putting dried leaves in the cup at the end of a ceramic tube, setting them on fire, and sucking in the smoke for pleasure and amusement.

Since it's only tangentially related to this tobacco issue, I won't rant—much—about the total illogicality and erroneousness of this whole scene, which is a stern warning to writers of HF about trying to transpose situations and/or mindsets from one point in history to another completely different point, simply because it's good stuff and it seems like a really cool scene to shoehorn into their story:

The fact is that the two princes were never "imprisoned" at all; they were residing under close protective guard, as any youthful members of the royal family would have been, in the secure and luxurious royal apartments in the Tower of London—*not* anywhere near the prison part of the Tower. The author of this disaster derived the scene directly from accounts of the imprisonment of the French royal family during the French Revolution, *three hundred years later* and under a totally different set of circumstances, when the French monarchy had been entirely abolished: the more sadistic or resentful of their keepers did get their kicks from harassing the ex-royals by, among other things, rudely blowing pipe smoke in their faces.

The Little Princes in the Tower in 1483-85, on the other hand—though no one will deny they must have been secretly murdered in the course of dynastic wars and a change of regime, either on the orders of their uncle, Richard III, or more likely on those of his successor, Henry VII—didn't have "jailers." And until the moment the secret order went out for their murder, they most definitely never had anti-royalist jailers who would have dared to deliberately insult or mistreat the sons of the popular late king or any other members of the very much extant and powerful English royal family.

A rough chronology of tobacco use in Europe:

Pipes, of various shapes, but the long-stemmed ones were most popular, were mostly used in the 1600s-1700s.

Primitive **cigars** were rolled by the smoker and smoked throughout this period on the European continent, but pipes were far more popular. Cigars became widespread and mass-manufactured in the 19th century.

Neither pipe nor cigar smokers inhale the smoke, which is extremely strong and harsh. Neither did smokers of early cigarettes, until milder forms of tobacco were developed in the early 20th century.

Cigarettes became common in the middle of the 19th century.

And if you've never smoked and don't really know the history of these nasty things, the essential differences between them are that cigars are always composed of whole tobacco leaves rolled into a cylinder, with a final tobacco leaf as the outer wrapping that holds it together; while cigarettes are much smaller, are made up of shredded tobacco, and use paper as the outer wrapping. In the 19th century, making cigarettes was a way to profit from the tobacco trimmings left over from cigar manufacturing. Victorian ragpickers and street urchins often earned a little money by collecting discarded cigar stubs in the gutters and selling the unburned parts by the pound to cigar or cigarette makers for recycling.

Note: Though fiction set in pre-1492 Europe and Asia is much more common than fiction set in the pre-Columbian Americas, should you be writing HF set among the Aztecs or the Navajo in the 13th century, you also need to know, of course, what *they* did and didn't eat, wear, use, interact with, and refer to before the Columbian Exchange. Many aspects of modern "traditional" Mexican cuisine, for example, are European imports—rice, cheese, sour cream, onions, olives, not to mention beef and chicken. Keep it in mind that no Native American—Inuit, Lakota, Navajo, Maya, Aztec, Inca, or anyone else—in either North or South America had heard of the following Eurasian foods and plants and plant products and animals (and many others) before 1492:

- Apples
- Bananas
- Carrots
- Cats (domestic)
- Cattle/dairy products
- Chickens (domestic)
- Citrus fruit
- Coffee
- Cotton
- Dandelions
- Donkeys
- Eggplant (aubergines)
- Flax (and linen)
- Garlic
- Geese (domestic)
- Goats (domestic)
- Honey (and honeybees)
- Horses
- Oats
- Olives/olive oil
- Onions
- Pigs (domestic)
- Rice

- Rye

- Sheep (domestic)

- Silk (and silkworms)

- Sugar (sugarcane)

- Tea

- Wheat

Your Grapes Weren't Flown in from Chile

You're a middle-class London housewife giving a dinner for friends in March 1560 and one of the highlights is a wonderful fruit bowl full of strawberries, peaches, and grapes.

What's wrong with this picture?

Strawberries, peaches, and grapes are all Old World fruits. Europeans had been eating them, when they could afford them, for centuries. So what's the problem?

Well, unless you were very, very wealthy and maintained a hothouse, until the mid 20th century you were never going to find fresh strawberries (which are ready to eat in late May or June), peaches (which are ripe in August), and grapes (which are ripe in September) all together in one bowl, particularly in March.

It's easy to forget how dependent we are today on modern conveniences, including supermarkets, refrigeration, and fast air or rail cargo shipping that can deliver out-of-season and exotic produce from warmer parts of the world to our dinner tables. But in past centuries, fresh fruits and vegetables were in season and available or they were not, and that was that. Nobody in New York in 1776 had strawberries in February that had been flown in from California or South America. Nobody but kings, dukes, and merchant princes in England in 1560 could have had strawberries and grapes at the same time. Even by 1930, very few ordinary people in Europe had ever eaten fresh pineapple. Read P. G. Wodehouse's hilarious short story "The Knightly Quest of Mervyn"[11] to see just how difficult and expensive it was to find out-of-season strawberries in London even in 1933.

And don't forget that it wasn't just fruit and vegetables that came with the seasons. In a century when nobody had a freezer, you ate fresh lamb in the spring or summer, while the lamb was still a lamb and hadn't yet grown into a sheep, because lambs are born in early spring. Roast lamb was traditional for Easter but never for Christmas. Stop a minute and remind yourself in what month your story is taking place before you put an out-of-season, and therefore unattainable, item on your character's plate.

Your Bonbons Haven't Been Invented Yet

It's also possible to get a food item or specific dish wrong simply because—like the problem with putting an electric light bulb in an Early Victorian gas-burning street lamp—its modern form hadn't quite been created yet. Many elegant dishes that we take for granted, especially fancy, involved ones like showy desserts, are the creations of the celebrity chefs of the

---

[11] In the collection *Mulliner Nights.*

19th and early 20th centuries, when fashionable restaurants grew common (see Chapter 15 for a brief history of the restaurant). If you've thought of having Madame de Pompadour start her formal dinner at Versailles in 1761 with vichyssoise, first look it up and you'll find that the classic, gourmet form of the chilled, puréed potato-and-leek-and-cream soup, despite the French name and seasonings, was actually invented (and *named*) by a French-born chef at the Ritz-Carlton Hotel in New York City in 1917.

Even Camembert, that quintessentially French variety of cheese, which you would think has been around since the Romans conquered Gaul, is actually a 19th-century creation, first made no earlier than 1790, perfected in the industrial era, and mass-produced only in the 1890s. (Being inexpensive to mass-produce, Camembert became part of French soldiers' standard rations during World War I. The American "doughboys" fighting in France first became aware of it then and, since every French soldier they met was eating it, automatically accepted it as a traditional French food of long, long standing.)

Look 'em up.

Some processed foods took a very long time to evolve to their present, familiar forms. For example: Chocolate (cacao, a plant product from the Americas, remember) as a hot drink had been very popular, though expensive, in western Europe since the mid 1600s, so we know for sure that hot cocoa was around in Paris in 1788, and so we can *assume* that chocolate was also a sweet treat . . . and at this point we're seeing, in our mind's eye, Marie-Antoinette dipping into a frilly rococo-style box of elegant chocolate bonbons, filled with nougat or nuts or vanilla cream, right?

Unfortunately not.

Marie-Antoinette never saw a chocolate bonbon in her life.

A clue here is that Europeans in the 17th and 18th centuries used the word "chocolate," without adjectives, to mean hot cocoa and nothing else ("the duchess took a cup of chocolate every morning"), because there was no other palatable way to consume cacao at the time.[12] In 1788, there was no such thing as chocolate candy, because the mechanical processes that turn raw cacao (which is bitter, oily, nasty stuff) into the smooth, sweet, rich, melting substance we eat in a chocolate bar hadn't yet been invented. 17th- and 18th-century hot *chocolat*—the drink—was made by whisking milk, water, and sugar with shavings from a hard block of ground cacao or with a slightly softer cacao paste, not with our familiar powdered cocoa; the processes that extract and separate the powder and the cocoa butter from the cacao pod wouldn't be invented until the 1810s and 20s. Until then, chocolate as a solid substance, even mixed with sugar, would have been oily, gritty, and definitely not very pleasant to eat—nobody was making it into gourmet candy.

Look up your processed foods. Chocolate candy is just one example of a highly processed food that bears no resemblance at all to the natural product it comes from. Always do your research to learn when distinctive dishes and modern methods of producing a particular food item were developed, because it's so very easy to make yet another anachronistic *faux pas* here.

---

[12] See Jim Chevallier's excellent website http://chezjim.com/18c/breakfast-18th.htm for a lengthy discussion of the 18th-century breakfast and the featured role that (hot) chocolate played in it.

7

Anachronisms: What's In a Name?

heesy "historical" romances from the 1970s and 80s are full of characters with the most improbable and exotic names, many of which, not surprisingly, are actually similar to the more florid names that you might have found in 1980s kindergartens or high school yearbooks. But before you go naming your medieval English heroine Brianna or Raelle or your Old West heroine Shawnée or Dominique, try a little research.

Given names, like everything else, go in and out of fashion. A popular name in 1970 may be one that people in 1870 had barely heard of, and people in 1770 had never even conceived of. People in past centuries, moreover, were much more conservative with names (and the spellings)—most were derived from religion or the region's traditional ethnic culture or legendary history, or inspired by celebrities (including royalty) or political movements of the time.

Your medieval English heroine (pre-1400), for example, was much more likely to have been named Mary, Margaret, Alys/Alice/Alison, Joan/Joanna, or Ann(e) than anything else, and her strapping hero was probably named Edward, Robert, Richard, Henry, Thomas, or John. A slightly later medieval/ Renaissance heroine could add Katherine, Jane, Elizabeth, and

Isabel to the list of hugely popular names, and her boyfriend might add George or Geoffrey or Charles or even Humphrey. Eleanor/Ellen was a popular medieval English name as well—but only after Eleanor of Aquitaine became queen of England in the 12th century, followed by later French or Spanish queens Eleanor of Provence (wife of Henry III) and Eleanor of Castile (first wife of Edward I).

This isn't to say there aren't exceptions. Not every Tudor lady was named Elizabeth or Jane, though the popular names were *very* popular (recall that three of Henry VIII's six wives were named Katherine). But if a Tudor baby girl's parents had chosen a less common name of the time, she was probably Frances or Bridget or Cecily or Arabella or Amy—not Shanna (strictly post-1960) or even Charlotte (common in England—because of George III's queen, Charlotte of Mecklenberg—in the 1700s and 1800s, but not before) or Christabel (Victorian) or Jennifer/Jenny (around for centuries, but wildly popular only in the 1960s/70s).

Medieval names all over Europe usually had religious origins; after the Reformation, however, English Protestants veered away from the most popular Catholic saints' names, such as Thomas, and often followed the growing trend of traditional Anglo-Saxon or Norman French names that were not religiously based, such as William or Robert. A century later, the Puritans, very strict Protestants, liked to name their children after virtues or exhortations—Mercy, Prudence, Faith, Charity, Forgive, Be-Faithful, Fear-the-Lord, and the like—or (the New Testament being too closely linked to Catholicism) characters from the Old Testament, such as Ruth, Sarah, Abigail, Esther, Jemima, Mehitabel, Nathan, Daniel, Moses, Abraham, Elijah, Jethro, Levi, Israel . . . and then there were the really unspellable and unpronounceable whoppers like Zipporah, Abishag, Jehoiachin, or Eliphalet.

In America, while trendier, but classically English, names like George, Charles, William, and Francis were continually creeping in, the standard Old Testament names like Samuel, Benjamin, and Josiah continued to be enormously popular among the Puritans' descendants in socially conservative colonial New England right through the 18th century. Take a look sometime at a list of the signers of the Declaration of Independence and you'll see mostly Old Testament names among the New Englanders, almost all traditional English names among the Southerners, and a mixture among those from the Mid-Atlantic.

Heading over to the Continent, 17th- or 18th-century French aristocrats and the well-read middle class, who usually had at least two given names and sometimes four or five, frequently had fancy-sounding medieval names (often of the more obscure and ancient Catholic saints—Blaise, Lambert, Hilaire, Roch, Benoît, etc.), with a few super-traditional saints' names (Marie, Jean, Anne) or other religiously oriented names (Toussaint, Pascal) thrown in for good measure, for a bit of holy insurance. (The Marquis de Lafayette's full string of given names: Marie-Joseph Paul Yves Roch Gilbert.) It's not hard to suspect that they, like most privileged classes throughout modern history, were consciously or unconsciously telling the world how much more cultured they were than the peasants who were all piously and unimaginatively named Marie, Jean, Jacques, Marie-Anne, Pierre, Marie-Jeanne, and so on.

But French names also go in and out of fashion like any others: Your lady in waiting to Marie-Antoinette (who was referred to as Antoinette, *not* Marie!) might have been named Gabrielle, Henriette, Adèle, Josèphe, or Sophie, but not Yvette or Danielle or Stéphanie or Mireille (a name that didn't even *exist* as a name before the 19th century)—names popular in

France since the middle of the 20th century, but not in the 18th. A look at the top fifty names for newborn girls in France in 2010 shows only nine that would have been among traditional names used in the 18th century, and very few religiously based names—the rest are trendy imports from other languages and cultures (Inès, Jade), fanciful modern creations (Océane, Ambre, Lilou), or regional names from the French provinces that would have been used only locally in previous centuries (Maëlys). So looking for 17th- or 18th-century French character names in the 2013 Marseilles or Dijon phone book simply won't do.

You also need to be sure that the names you choose for your characters are appropriate for their social class. As I mentioned above, the upper classes were usually more imaginative and varied in choosing names for their children, whether out of a far richer intellectual and cultural education, or just plain snobbery. The Victorian upper classes in both Britain and America, for instance, often went for elaborate names for girls, often taken from history or literature or mythology (Lavinia, Araminta, Lucinda, Evangeline, India, Melissa, Julia,

Amelia), and very traditional, classic (sometimes medieval or ancient Roman) names for boys (James, Edward, William, Lionel, Marcus, Augustus, etc.) Another snobbish British trend by the late 18th century was to use aristocratic surnames— not necessarily the names of anyone related to the namer, though—as given names for boys (Percy, Howard, Neville, Dudley, Cecil, Stanley, Herbert, and many more, all of which are or were the family surnames of prominent British noble houses that dated from the Middle Ages or Tudor era).

The Victorian lower middle class and working class also began to break away from the traditional, usually religiously based names that had been common for centuries and went for fancier-sounding names for girls, but since they weren't reading all the novels and ancient history that the upper classes were, the "fancier" names they chose were more often names of flowers or gems (Daisy, Violet, Ruby). Untold thousands of working-class Victorian and Edwardian boys in Britain were named Albert, which had been a very uncommon name in England until Prince Albert's marriage to Queen Victoria in 1840, but although it was the name of the Prince Consort, it was less often given among the upper classes. (Oddly, fewer working-class girls than you might think were named Victoria at the time.)

So, for your story set in 1550 or 1880, instead of impulsively giving your English or American heroine the lovely, romantic, but totally inappropriate name "Dominique"—which was, unfortunately, not even in the Top Thousand of popular names among English speakers until the last third of the 20th century (and was mostly a French *male* name until quite recently)—how do you find the right, period-appropriate, names for your characters, wherever and whenever they may be from?

Well, first of all, if you've been doing the proper research for your story, you've probably run across lots of names of historical figures of the time and place. Read enough and you'll develop an automatic sense of what was a name of the period and what wasn't. If you've been reading biographies of some influential people from your chosen period (and I strongly suggest that you do, even if all your characters are totally fictional), you'll find loads and loads of names of both important and peripheral people. You may not need to know anything about somebody's mother-in-law, for example, but you can always lift her given name if it's an interesting one! Run your eye down the index columns of any thick biography and you'll find dozens of names there for the borrowing (mix up given names and surnames, of course, so you don't inadvertently give a character the name of a lesser historical figure whom someone moderately familiar with the period will immediately recognize).

Don't, however, attempt to make up glamorous-sounding names or get kreatyv with the spelling of a classic given name, even for your wildly romantic heroes and heroines, unless you want some snickers among your readers; no Elizabethan was ever named Mayree or Eddwyrd "just to be different." Naming was conservative, as mentioned previously, and an off-beat version of a name in a past century, until, perhaps, the over-ornate mid-Victorian age, usually implied only that the person giving the odd name was a bad speller.

A general note: *Don't*, whatever you do, rely solely on a name-the-baby book to find interesting names for your historical characters. They are pretty much useless for this. While they may tell you the origin of a name and what it meant, possibly a couple of thousand years ago in ancient Hebrew or something, what they won't tell you is a name's use history, when and where it was first recorded as used, and when and where it may have become popular and then went out of fashion. Using a baby name book as your sole source will probably lead to disastrous name anachronisms if you're not very, very careful.

On the other hand, **www.behindthename.com/** is a terrific online resource for name statistics in the U.S., and sometimes elsewhere, since 1880, and a source of common given names all over the world (but, alas, not always with hints as to their histories).

Ancient Roman names

The Romans, while they were very good at many things—war, architecture, plumbing—weren't terribly outstanding in the imagination department when it came to language, literature, or . . . names. But the Romans, particularly the upper crust, had definite rules for naming their children, and if you name your patrician Roman heartthrob just "Marcus" (with no other names) or your Roman heroine "Ellena" or "Parthia," eyebrows are going to be raised.

The grossly oversimplified essentials: You can break an ancient Roman (male) upper-class citizen's name down into three parts: a given ("first") name (*praenomen*), a clan name (*gens*), and a "nickname" or "family branch" name (*cognomen*—although not every Roman patrician had one or used one). This can become confusing for us because it became fashionable for Europeans and Americans in the 18th and 19th centuries to name their children after ancient Roman heroes; but a Victorian gentleman who decided to give his eldest son a classical name usually gave the baby a Roman *gens* as the baby's given name, and by now many of those clan names—Julius, Horatius, Claudius, Cornelius, etc.—sound like first names to us, instead of like the Jones and Biggs and MacIntosh and Smedley and so on that they were to the ancient Romans.

And just how imagination-deficient were the aristocratic Romans in naming their children? Well, by the first century B.C. there were only about twelve or fifteen *praenomina* (first names) available for males, period. Marcus, Lucius, Publius, Gaius, Gnaeus were among the popular ones; also (if you needed additional demonstration of the lack-of-imagination department) Secundus, Tertius, Quintus, Sextus, Septimus, Octavius, and Decimus—Second, Third, Fifth, Sixth, Seventh, Eighth, and Tenth, which didn't necessarily refer to birth order within the family, but may have originally referred to the month in which the child was born (Septimus born in September, for example. How sentimental is that? "Ah, my dear Seventh, my beloved son, I couldn't come up with a better name for you . . .").

Male *praenomina* weren't used except among immediate family members and intimate friends (so think long and hard before you have any character except an intimate friend or family member address a Roman patrician as "Publius" or "Marcus" rather than by his *gens*). They also gradually dropped out of sight in documents, which is why we're so used to hearing the name "Julius Caesar" and thinking that "Julius" was his given name. Julius Caesar's given name wasn't Julius, it was Gaius, though only his immediate family would have called him Gaius, and probably nobody ever dared to be that familiar with him after he began taking over the Roman world. Julius was the *gens*, the family name, meaning "of the clan Julii"— and "Caesar[13]" was the *cognomen*, the family branch name— it means "a head of hair" and the branch was undoubtedly des-

cended from some early Roman of the Julii who was particularly well known for his great hair. (Which must have felt a bit ironic for the balding Gaius Julius Caesar.) Essentially, you can translate the name as "Gaius, of the clan Julii, the Hairy."

Some *cognomina* were distinctly unflattering. Ancient Greek historian Plutarch related the origin of the *cognomen* of orator and writer Marcus Tullius Cicero: "The Latins call a chickpea 'Cicer,' and a cleft or dent at the tip of his nose,

---

[13] Actually pronounced "KYE-sahr," to rhyme with "pie car", not the Anglicized "SEE-zer".

which resembled the cleft in a chickpea, gave [the family branch's ancestor] the surname of Cicero." This was one of the odder ones, but other, even less flattering, *cognomina* attached to many different clans included Balbus ("Stutterer") and Naso ("Nosy," probably referring to an oversized nose).

Dictator Lucius Cornelius Sulla Felix, known to contemporaries and history just as Sulla, was "Lucius, of the clan Cornelii, the Red-Complexioned (*Sulla*) and Happy/Lucky (*Felix*)"—essentially he was going by "Ruddy." "Augustus," on the other hand, which we're familiar with as the name of the first Roman emperor, was not a name at all, though we've made it one over the centuries; it was a title of respect bestowed on Gaius Octavius (no *cognomen*), the guy we usually know as "Octavian" from movies about Cleopatra. The title "Augustus" was given him by the Senate, a couple of years after he'd made himself First Citizen of Rome, so he finally became—having dropped his original *gens* "Octavius" and taken up "Julius" from his great-uncle Julius Caesar, who'd formally adopted him into the Julii in his will—Gaius Julius Caesar Augustus: "Gaius, of the clan Julii, the Hairy (*Caesar*) and the Eminent (*Augustus*)."

And girls' names? What were the popular girls' names of ancient Rome?

While I'm grossly oversimplifying again here, to be strictly accurate, by the time of the late Republic and the Empire, there *were* no official girls' given names among patrician (aristocratic) citizens.

Girls from important families, reflecting ancient Roman society's dismissive view of women compared to men, were given a single name, a feminized form of the father's *gens* (by replacing the ending "-us" with "-ia" or "-a"), and that was that. Even if they had five sisters. It was as if, in the modern USA, all of John Smith's daughters were named "Smithia" and nothing else—no last name, no nuthin'.

Gaius Julius Caesar's daughter was automatically named Julia . . . and if he'd had five daughters, *all* of them would have been named Julia. Augustus (Gaius *Julius* Caesar Augustus, remember, formerly Gaius Octavius) had one daughter, also automatically Julia, while his sister was Octavia. Marcus Antonius—Mark Antony, to use the annoying traditional Anglicization of his name—had, by his two Roman wives, three daughters, all of whom were of course named Antonia. Families individualized their daughters by giving them nicknames (which might evolve from the girl's physical characteristics, such as Flavia, "golden," for the color of her hair; her habits or likes; or, for instance, applying the Greek name Helen to a remarkably beautiful girl) or by calling them Minor (the second or younger daughter, also Secunda), Tertia (the third daughter), and so on. Women who went by their nicknames may have gone by them all their lives, and might accumulate some titles that would attach to their names, but officially they were still Cornelia (daughter of the Cornelius family), or Pompeia Minor (younger daughter of the Pompeius family), or Claudia Tertia (third daughter of the Claudius family), etc.

In short, if you simply must give an aristocratic ancient Roman female character an exotic, fanciful name that doesn't derive from her father's clan name, do mention the fact that it's one of those frequent nicknames and that her real, official name is something realistic that reflects actual Roman naming.

8

Ānachronisms: Guns

don't pretend to be an expert on guns. If you are a military history or firearms enthusiast and know all about types and manufactures and makers of guns, and their history, you can skip right ahead past this part.

If you're not, and have never held a gun and have no interest whatsoever in guns except for using them because you have to as occasional props in your HF, then the first thing you need to do, in order to avoid silly mistakes that will send gun enthusiasts into fits of hysterical laughter, is to memorize this sentence and keep in mind the following oversimplified but essential basic guidelines:

Though they both refer to handguns, the words "pistol" and "revolver" are NOT synonymous or interchangeable.

Pistols are old (before the 1820s). Revolvers are new(ish) (after 1814).

Pistols and revolvers

Any handgun used before 1814 must be a single-shot **pistol** of some type. A pistol needs to be reloaded after each shot (except for pistols with multiple barrels—but each *barrel* still needs to be reloaded after each shot). Pistols are muzzle-loaders (from the front, meaning the business end, of the barrel)— you load them by ramming a ball and charge and wadding of some type down the length of the barrel, using a ramrod that is always, when not in use, attached to the pistol below the barrel for convenience.

The first true **revolver**—a handgun with one barrel that has a *revolving* cylinder and multiple chambers for projectiles, which allows you to shoot up to (usually) six times before reloading—was invented in 1814. Its firing mechanism was a flintlock, the same as was used on 17th- and 18th-century pistols and muskets. The percussion cap revolver, which made for more reliable firing and made the revolver much more popular and common, was invented in 1836 (by Samuel Colt, hence the Colt revolver, familiar from countless Westerns). In general, revolvers are breech-loading (from the rear of the barrel)—in other words, you open your revolver by the grip, pop your bullets or cartridges into the chambers of the cylinder, and snap it back together again.

Of course, people didn't all immediately mothball their pistols in 1815 or even 1836 and rush out to buy revolvers as soon as they were invented. Pistols continued to be used for decades, especially in Europe, where a sidearm was a far less essential part of one's getup than it was on the American frontier, and handguns—after street lighting improved—were used mostly for dueling. It's perfectly possible that someone in the last third of the 19th century, especially someone poor or someone living in a remote, backward area of Europe, might be well behind the times and still have his grandfather's old flintlock pistol around the house for emergencies.

But it doesn't work the other way: **Revolvers (six-shooters) belong to the 1800s and DO NOT belong anywhere in previous centuries.** 17th-century pirates and 18th-century adventurers carried pistols, while 19th-century cowboys and cattle rustlers carried revolvers. If your French musketeer or Georgian highwayman is packing something that you call a "revolver," you might as well go all the way and give him a phaser from *Star Trek*; it wouldn't be much more historically inaccurate.

Pistols could range in size from "horse pistols" a foot or more long, which fired a bullet large enough to put down a wounded horse with one shot; to pocket pistols, used mostly as a concealed weapon for self-defense on dark 17th- or 18th-century streets, which could be just a few inches long with a very small caliber bullet. The paranoid might carry a pocket pistol with two or three or four barrels, each barrel loaded and ready—just in case. Double-barreled pistols, however, could be dangerous, often misfiring (not going off when they should) or both barrels going off at the same time, or exploding in the shooter's hand, so carrying multiple small pistols was a more common practice. (To use your double-barreled pistol: after firing one barrel, you grab the whole barrel section— it'll be warm but not too hot to touch—and twist it around so that the second barrel connects with the firing mechanism, like twisting a spray bottle's squirter from "spray" to "stream.")

Flintlock pistol: The hammer, which often
looks a lot like a duck's head and grips the flint in
the duck's bill, is at left, the steel at right

The flintlock was the most efficient and common type of firing mechanism for both pistols and muskets in the 17th, 18th, and early 19th centuries (previous centuries used the more primitive matchlock or wheellock; the flintlock was superseded by the factory-made percussion cap around 1840). A flintlock uses a chip of flint that is gripped in a pincer-like affair (the hammer) on top of the gun. When the hammer is cocked and the trigger is squeezed, the hammer, propelled by a spring, snaps violently forward and the flint strikes a spark from a steel plate (the steel or battery), which ignites the charge in the "pan" (remember "a flash in the pan"?) where a little priming gunpowder is waiting, and the resulting tiny explosion ignites the main charge in the barrel and makes the pistol or musket go off.

Muskets and rifles

The main difference between muskets and rifles, for the basic purposes of HF, is that a rifle is accurate but takes a considerable time to load properly; while a musket, in the hands of a shooter who's had practice, and with premeasured cartridges available, can be reloaded relatively quickly, but can barely hit the broad side of a barn.

Once again—although muskets and rifles, unlike pistols and revolvers, co-existed for a few centuries—**the two words are not synonymous or interchangeable**.

Primitive **rifles** were around since the 1400s. Rifles have a tight, spiral grooved ("rifled") barrel that makes the projectile spin and sends it on a straight, accurate trajectory; while muskets ("smoothbores") have no rifling and are far less accurate. The technology was improved during the 18th century, but until the mid 19th century, all rifles were muzzle-loaders and had to be loaded just right, with the bullet and the charge packed down very tightly in the barrel, which takes a few minutes. Although much more efficient breech-loading rifles were notorious during the U.S. Civil War, here a muzzle-loading hunting rifle is still in use on the midwestern American frontier around 1871:

> Now [Pa] was ready to load the gun again. ... Laura handed him the smooth, polished cow horn full of gunpowder. The top of the horn was a metal cap.
> Pa filled this cap full of the gunpowder and poured the powder down the barrel of the gun. Then he shook the

gun a little and tapped the barrel, to be sure that all the powder was together in the bottom. "Where's my patch box?" he asked them, and Mary gave him the little tin box full of little pieces of greased cloth. Pa laid one of these bits of greasy cloth over the muzzle of the gun, put one of the shiny new bullets on it, and with the ramrod he pushed the bullet and the cloth down the gun barrel. Then he pounded them tightly against the powder. When he hit them with the ramrod, the ramrod bounced up in the gun barrel, and Pa caught it and thrust it down again. He did this for a long time.

Next he put the ramrod back in its place against the gun barrel. Then taking a box of caps from his pocket, he raised the hammer of the gun and slipped one of the little bright caps over the hollow pin that was under the hammer. He let the hammer down, slowly and carefully. If it came down quickly—bang!—the gun would go off.

... Whenever he shot at a wild animal, he had to stop and load the gun—measure the powder, pour it in and shake it down, put in the bullet and pound them down, and then put a fresh cap under the hammer—before he could shoot again.

[from *Little House in the Big Woods*
by Laura Ingalls Wilder[14]]

A hastily or carelessly loaded rifle misfires when you try to use it, or explodes in your face. The length of time required to load them properly made rifles impractical for use in warfare by anyone but sharpshooters (i.e. snipers). Don't expect your hero, when suddenly attacked by the villain or a hungry puma, to be able to get off more than one shot if all he's got with him is his trusty muzzle-loading rifle. By the time the hero has reloaded his rifle, the villain will have completed his villainy (or your hero is the puma's lunch).

---

[14] The autobiographical *Little House* books, first published in the 1930s, are an invaluable resource for details of American frontier life in the Midwest and Great Plains in the 1870s and 1880s. Forget everything about the TV series.

Muskets, on the other hand, are more primitive, cheaper to make, faster to load, and were used by the infantry in warfare from the 17th century through the first third of the 19th century. No one went hunting with a musket unless he was loading it with small shot (in which case it was usually called a "fowling piece"). You'd never get close enough to your deer or rabbit to be able to hit the critter with a single musket ball with a reasonable expectation of accuracy.

Flintlock muskets are easy to load because, without the tight, rifled barrel, they don't require anything like the length of time that a muzzle-loading rifle does. The lack of rifling and the slightly wider barrel that allow quick loading, however, let the bullet (actually a round musket ball) rattle just a tiny bit as it's shooting down the barrel, and this can skew the bullet's direction significantly by the end of its flight. A gun with such unpredictable accuracy, or lack of it, is no use for target shooting, but will do for very short range and/or the crowded arena of a battlefield; the ball that was shot at one soldier in a mass volley usually missed him but hit someone else nearby.

(Just to confuse you further: Pistols, from the 18th century and before, were smoothbores like muskets—the lack of accuracy was rarely an issue at close range—but rifled one-shot pistols did exist in the 19th century, especially for dueling, though using them was often considered cheating.)

A musket, like all muzzle-loaders, used balls and loose powder; a musket "cartridge" resembled a modern cartridge only in its rough shape. Musket cartridges were little hand-folded paper packets or tubes that held a measured amount of black powder and one musket ball. To use them, you tore the cartridge open, usually with your teeth, if you were in the midst of battle; poured a little bit of powder into the firing pan to prime it so that the flintlock's spark would have something to ignite; poured the rest of the powder down the barrel; scrunched the ball into the empty, crumpled paper cartridge (for wadding, to ensure a tighter fit) and pushed that into the barrel; and rammed it all in with a couple of good hard shoves of your ramrod, and you were ready to fire again. An 18th-century soldier who'd been well drilled could shoot and reload in fifteen to twenty seconds, getting off three or four shots a minute.

The mid 19th century put an end to the old-fashioned musket with great improvements to the breech-loading rifle, a gun that combined the most useful and practical aspects of both musket and rifle. (Crude breech-loaders had been around since the 1400s, but were quite rare.) Effective breech-loaders were developed in the first half of the 19th century, in tandem with the self-contained (metal) ammunition cartridge. By the time of the U.S. Civil War, a breech-loading infantry gun was both easy to reload (as fast as a musket) and as accurate as a rifle—which was partly responsible for the horrific number of casualties of the Civil War.

This one's the revolver…

Basic Rules
You Need To Keep In Mind
That Will Help You Avoid
the Silly Mistakes

General Rule
No. 3

Do Not Borrow Your Period Details & Information From Other People's Historical Novels & Movies

hy?

Because sometimes their authors get stuff wrong. (*Sometimes?*) OK, often they get stuff wrong. Especially movies. Especially Hollywood movies. Do not trust a Hollywood/commercial movie to get more than 50% of its historical facts and/or details right, intentionally or not—for any of a number of reasons, including:

• "Even if X never happened and couldn't possibly have happened, it makes a better story told our way." [*Braveheart*—William Wallace's movie fling with French hottie Princess Isabelle, although the historical Isabelle was ten years old at the time of Wallace's death and had not yet arrived in England; her son, King Edward III—who, it is insinuated in the movie, was fathered by Wallace—was born seven years after Wallace died.]

• "Our star/director/costume designer thinks the genuine period hairstyle/gown is really lame and insists on having the heroine's hair/gown styled so that it looks like the cover of last month's *Vogue*." [any Hollywood movie made between

1915 and 1975, though they've been getting better about this during the past few decades. Movies made in the 1940s and 50s are probably the very worst offenders—their 17th- or 18th-century heroines tend to have hair/makeup that looks as if it came off Betty Grable or Eva Peròn, and "period" gowns that look like prom dresses from *Grease*.]

• "We know these events actually happened over the course of ten years, but it makes a much tighter movie if it looks as if it all happened within six months or so." [*Elizabeth*—the one with Cate Blanchett. Or *The King's Speech*, or many more.]

• "The average idiot with a high-school education and fourth-grade reading level who'll see our movie already 'knows' (*assumes*) that Scots have always worn kilts, so we'll have our thirteenth-century Scots wear plaid kilts even though some nerd has just told us that kilts weren't worn until the sixteenth century or later." [*Braveheart*, of course.]

• "It's simpler in the script and cheaper for the budget to combine these two events/characters/locations into one event/character/location." [nearly every historical movie ever made.]

and, of course,

• "Except for a couple of eggheads, who gives a s*** if it's accurate anyway?"

There are a few exceptions. You can probably trust almost any nautical detail you see in the movie *Titanic*, for instance, because director James Cameron has proved himself to be as obsessed with the ship and the history of the fatal voyage and getting the minor details right as any dedicated author of HF—though there *is* that dime with FDR on it that every nitpicker loves to point out . . . But these exceptions are very, very rare.

Don't rely on movies for historical accuracy.
Ever.
But don't count on doing your research of an era and its

daily life by reading other people's HF, either. As we know, all historical novelists make mistakes—some many more than others—and you don't want to end up borrowing details from one of the clueless novelists who makes howler after howler, do you?

By HF I mean, of course, fiction set a good chunk of time (half a century or more) previous to the date it's written—a novelist's depiction and interpretation of a previous era that the novelist him/herself has probably not experienced. Thus Charles Dickens's novels, which are all—except for *A Tale of Two Cities* and *Barnaby Rudge*—set in Dickens's contemporary early- and mid-Victorian world, are not "historical fiction" but period classics. Dickens was writing about and describing the world around him, with all the ordinary details of everyday life, technology, customs, and society that he knew well, just as chick-lit authors today are writing about the upscale life in 21st-century New York City that they, presumably, have experienced in one way or another. (In 2248, authors of HF will undoubtedly be reading 21st-century chick-lit for details about *our* remote and exotic world. "Just think of living at a time that was so primitive that compu-municators weren't implanted into their ear canals and brainstems at birth!")

A Tale of Two Cities and *Barnaby Rudge*, however, written in the mid 19th century but set in the 18th century, respectively twenty and thirty years before Dickens was born, are true HF. (And Dickens, just like thousands of other authors of HF, had to research the period to write them, and got stuff wrong.) So while a 21st-century author, writing a historical novel set in 1855 London, will find a gold mine of perfect period information, details, and atmosphere in any of Dickens's contemporary novels, somebody writing about the French Revolution should *not* rely on Dickens's depiction of it in *A Tale of Two Cities* for her research. (Please, please, *don't*, I beg you!)

Relying on other people's historical novels is deceiving. They're probably going to get the big, important facts right, because the major facts are easy to look up and the authors don't have any valid, pressing reason, such as a movie's length or budget, to change them. So a novel about Elizabeth I is probably going to get the dates of her birth, her coronation, and the Spanish Armada right. If it doesn't get those obvious dates right, a sharp-eyed editor will probably reject it long before it ever reaches print.

What a novel about Elizabeth, or featuring Elizabeth, may very well get *wrong* is the same minor stuff that *you're* potentially going to get wrong if you assume too much—all the details of lesser events and daily life which plenty of people make errors over, which you want to get right in your novel, which I'm discussing individually in this book because so many people do get them wrong. If you read a novel set in the court of Elizabeth I, and read a scene in which her ladies in waiting are sipping afternoon tea (as I read once in someone's rather perfunctorily researched romance—"*Nobody will notice . . .*"), you'd better not *assume* that 16th-century English aristocrats drank tea just because you know that (1) English people drink lots of tea *now*; (2) they also drink gallons of tea in Jane Austen's novels written in the 1800s and 1810s; and (3) because you saw Elizabeth's ladies taking afternoon tea in somebody else's novel written in 1988.

(Elizabethans *didn't* drink tea—or coffee either—and probably had barely heard of them except as exotic Oriental medicinal herbs; the rich began to adopt both in the mid to late 1600s, at least half a century after Elizabeth's death. And the custom of getting together for "afternoon tea" with a light meal of finger foods and pastries is said to have been started around 1840 by the Duchess of Bedford, one of Queen Victoria's ladies in waiting. Go look up the history of tea and coffee in Wikipedia.)

And when your aristocratic 16th-century French heroine gets engaged and everybody celebrates, you shouldn't simply *assume*, as another author did, that since the French invented champagne, they would have drunk it in 1573, wouldn't they? (Nor should you assume as the makers of the otherwise excellent 1970s *Three/Four Musketeers* movies did, when they gave our heroes champagne in 1625.) Because champagne, no matter what that author and that screenwriter believed and wrote, was developed in the mid-1600s and became well-known and popular around 1700. Look it up . . .

Don't pluck your neat little details of everyday life and custom in a given historical period from somebody else's novel and put them in your own without checking them and double-checking them first. Which means, basically, do your own research: don't copy someone else's research—or, very possibly, lack of it.

Never assume!

9

Money Bloopers: Getting the Coinage, Prices, & Values Right

ack around 1980, a production company made yet another remake (a TV-movie) of *A Tale of Two Cities*.[15] It turned out to be an unnecessary, extremely boring, and actually quite bad remake for so many, many reasons, which I won't go into. But when I watched it again, a long time after 1980, after I'd been absorbing details about late-18th-century France for twenty-plus years, one minor detail they'd casually included nearly made me do one of those cliché'd sitcom moments where someone does a double-take at something and sprays his coffee across the room.

I'm sure the screenwriter was doing his best to sound authentic by dropping the name of a genuine item from the history books into his script. But cleverly trying to sound authentic when you don't really know what you're talking about (*"Nobody will notice . . ."*) is a sure recipe for a howler in historical fiction—or "historical" movie-making.

Recall the plot of *A Tale of Two Cities*: Sydney Carton,

---

[15] Made for Hallmark Hall of Fame and starring Chris Sarandon in the dual roles of Sydney Carton and Charles Darnay.

determined to save Charles Darnay from the guillotine, goes to an apothecary's shop and buys a mysterious substance with which he'll drug Charles into unconsciousness. (We won't even go into the original big honking anachronism in the novel that many literary critics have pointed out over the decades, that Mr. Dickens, in a story set in the 1780s/90s, was clearly referring to chloroform—which wasn't discovered until the 1830s and wasn't commonly used until the 1850s[16] . . . Once again, Do *Not Borrow Your Period Information From Other People's Historical Novels and Movies*, even Great Literary Classics.)

In this particular filming of the tale, Carton is shown going to the shop and buying the drug. "Fourteen louis, citizen," says the apothecary, handing the bottle over.

Fourteen louis??? I said to myself, once the spraying-the-coffee-across-the-room moment was over.

Because no little bottle of a mysterious knockout drug, even a yet-to-be-invented one, or indeed anything at all that was for sale in an 18th-century Parisian apothecary shop, should have—or ever did—cost several thousand dollars.

A wise scriptwriter would have avoided the mention of specific prices and coinage altogether (as Dickens did in the novel by mumbling vaguely about "gold" now and then) and just showed Carton pushing a couple of small coins across the counter. Unfortunately, this writer had read a book or two and felt he had to show off. But if he had done a little serious homework, rather than just seeing the "louis" coin mentioned somewhere in a book about 18th-century France and probably exclaiming "Aha! A coin name I can throw around, and who'll know the difference?", he would have found out just how much a louis was actually worth—in other words, what you could buy with one in 1793. ("Louis," by the way, is short for *louis d'or*, or "gold louis," called so because the king's head was on the gold coin and there had been kings named

---

[16] John Sutherland, "Where does Sydney Carton get his chloroform?", also in *Who Betrays Elizabeth Bennet? Further Puzzles in Classic Fiction*.

Louis on the French throne in unbroken succession since 1610.)

What the script probably should have said was "fourteen sous"—a sou being worth, in purchasing power, roughly between 50 cents and $1 (or more) in 2013 U.S. money (depending upon what you were buying: before mass production and cheap shipping, manufactured/processed or imported goods cost proportionally a lot more than they do now). In late-18th-century France, twenty sous made a livre, and twenty-four livres made a louis d'or. I won't even go into the complications of the inflation and the devalued paper money of 1793 that made gold coins far more desirable and valuable than usual. Do your multiplication, using a sou at an average 75 cents, and you'll find that:

1 sou (.75) x 20 = 1 livre ($15)
1 livre ($15) x 24 = 1 louis d'or ($360)
14 x 1 louis ($360) = $5,040 in 2013 U.S. dollars.

Fourteen louis? Yikes. I sincerely doubt Carton had the equivalent of five thousand dollars in his pocket. Don't you?

Want more of this nonsense? In the same movie, the script-writer, who was apparently in love with the word "louis" but seemed to think that a louis was worth about forty-two cents, has the sinister French guards at the barrier on the road charge Charles Darnay a fee for his escort to Paris. Oh, those evil, evil French revolutionaries. How much is it going to cost poor Charles?

Would you believe, according to the script, that his escort would cost him "a hundred louis" (that's roughly $36,000 today)?

And then, just to compound the absurdity, Charles sourly hands over what looks like three or four small coins, rather than the fat, heavy little sack of gold that would have been a hundred louis. (Obviously the director wasn't even paying attention—honestly, guys, if you're going to specify a hundred whatevers, it should *look* onscreen like a hundred of them and not like three of them, shouldn't it?) Oh, dear, oh, *dear*. Hack filmmakers who want to make period films shouldn't be allowed out alone.

Unfortunately, it's not just movies that are guilty of this kind of error: An extremely inept novel set in 18th-century France, discussed previously in the "Dialogue" chapter, manages, among many other howlers, to mention that people were paying fifty livres ($750) for a sack of potatoes (whether or not bourgeois Parisian families were routinely eating potatoes or finding them at the markets at this time is open to question) and one louis (yes, $360) for a single copy of a newspaper . . .

A very nice man who came to one of my readings bought one of my novels, devoured it, and phoned me a couple of days later to tell me how much he'd liked it. "But," he added, quite kindly, "where you mention that there were three livres to an écu . . . actually there were six."

"Oh?" I said, because I'd looked that up, of course, and some history books had said three livres to the silver écu, and some had said six, and I'd had to choose one or the other. "Are you sure?"

I then mentioned that I'd taken, as my clinching source material, a line from a genuine journal from the 1780s in which the narrator said he'd thrust a three-livre coin in his pocket before going out one night.

"There were half-écu coins, too," the nice man told me, apologetically. "That's what he would have been referring to. But it was six livres to the écu. I collect coins, you see, and I just looked it up in So-and-So's book on 18th-century European coinage, just to be sure."

Oh. Right.

Oh well! I'll fix it in a future edition . . .

~ ~ ~ ~ ~

I provide the above anecdotes merely to illustrate how easy it is to make dumb mistakes over money and coinage in your historical fiction. And a coinage error is not one of those mistakes that will be noticed only by the six history geeks and Ph.D.s in the world who are obsessed with a particular super-obscure subject. A lot of people collect, or at least are fascinated by, historic coins, and there are a lot of books and websites out there on the subject of ancient, medieval, and pre-19th-century coinage. The coin collectors may be less aware of an antique coin's essential buying power in the period when it was in circulation, but still . . . you probably should try to get all of it right.

So, the moral of these stories? You need to know your money, the currency of the time and place of your HF. Don't just grab a few romantic-sounding names of coins out of the history narrative you're reading and think that randomly mentioning them will do for your story background when you need somebody to buy something. (*"Nobody will notice . . ."*)

No matter how much you may be tempted to, you can't, unfortunately, get away with completely dodging the issue. While moviemakers can and should limit themselves to showing coins onscreen but not talking about them, writers of fiction have to be specific in order to create a believable world, complete with trade and money. Saving yourself tedious research by never being precise about the coinage, particularly in dialogue, produces incredibly lame results:

> Mother opened her hanging pocket and took out a silver coin. "Here's some money for a bit of gingerbread," she said.
>
> "And here's another coin for some marchpane," added Father.
>
> * * *
>
> "I have three silver coins to spend," announced Ruth.
>
> "I have only two silver pieces," Susanna said. ... She finally spent her second coin for a needle for her mother.
>
> * * *
>
> "Have you silver?" [the gypsy] asked. . . . Ruth opened her pocket and drew out her last coin. . . . The woman tucked the

coin into the gay pocket that hung at her side.

* * *

The gypsy woman turned to Susanna. "Come, dearie, let me tell your fortune."

"Oh, no, ma'am, thank you," Susanna said. "I have no more money. I spent my last coin for a needle for my mother."

[From *Susanna's Candlestick* by Lillie V. Albrecht]

Jeepers. This barefaced example of skipping the research and ending up with stilted, phony dialogue is, alas, from an otherwise very good historical children's book written by my grandmother and published in 1970. It's possible, of course,

that her editor dumbed down the vocabulary from "penny" or "halfpenny" to "coin," feeling that American children would be confused if they read about an English "penny" in the 17th century—made of silver and worth a few bucks by today's standards—and tried to relate it to a 1970 American copper penny. But it's rarely a good idea to condescend to your readers, even kids.

Wouldn't you rather read about a silver halfpenny than something as vague as a "coin"? And do you ever ask a friend if he has a "coin" when you're fishing in your change purse to feed the parking meter? No, you ask him if he has a quarter or a dime or a nickel. Everybody knows what their local coins of various denominations are called, whether dimes or groats or halfpennies or thalers or denarii or ducats. Don't think we can't tell you're dodging the issue!

So you need to know (for example) that in London in 1875, four farthings made a penny, and twelve pence made a shilling, and twenty shillings made a pound, though the gold coin that was worth a pound was called a sovereign, not a pound (and twenty-*one* shillings made a guinea, which was a unit but not a coin by the late 19th century, though guinea coins were around in the 18th century and earlier)—and, what's more, that an English penny and an American penny didn't have anything like the same value at the time, and that, in purchasing power, or what you could buy with it, an English penny in 1875 was a lot closer to a 21st-century U.S. dollar than to a 21st-century cent.

The best source for this kind of information is not regular history books. Sure, a history book, or any Brit who was born before 1960, will tell you how many shillings there were to a British pound before they decimalized the currency in 1971. But it probably won't tell you, unless it's a highly technical and dry scholarly work about economics, commodities, and the wholesale price per bushel of something or other in 1880, what and how much you could actually buy for your shilling in, say, 1714 or 1860 or 1938. For this, you need to go back to original sources, if you can—bills and record books; diaries; letters; advertisements in newspapers; even fiction or drama from the period you're researching (*from* the period, not *about* the period—*Do Not Borrow Your Information From Other People's Historical Novels and Movies*). It is, naturally, easier to find this material if you're researching a period within the last four or five centuries, so people who want to know the purchasing power of an ancient Athenian coin are probably going to have to do a lot more detective work.

Say you want to know the purchasing power of English money in the 1840s. Well, go download *A Christmas Carol* from Project Gutenberg, if it isn't already on your bookshelf. Dickens tells us in this 1847 novelette exactly how much Bob Cratchit earns as Ebenezer Scrooge's clerk: fifteen shillings per week—for which he'd have worked six days a week, not five, and probably nine or ten hours a day.

We can tell, from everything else Dickens says about Scrooge's tight-fisted ways, that it's not very much, and that Bob just barely manages to support a wife and large family on it (with some help from what the older children earn—child labor is quite common). So we know Bob's pay is a stingy and barely-sufficient salary for the time, probably the equivalent of a modern "minimum wage" McDonald's salary for what was actually a lower-middle-class office job.

So take your American minimum wage (which varies from state to state, but try a rough average), say $8 per hour in 2013. A minimum-wage worker at $8 per hour earns $320 for a 40-hour week before taxes.

$320 / 15 = $21.33

Divide $320 by Bob's weekly wage of fifteen shillings and you get about $21 in 2013—the essential value, in pay and purchasing power, of a single 1847 shilling (which, by the way, makes an 1847 British penny the equivalent of about $1.75 today, and an 1847 pound about $425.00). And now you know that a shilling, though it was roughly 13 U.S. cents in 1970, was a substantial amount of money in 1847 and you won't cluelessly write a scene in which you have your fictional 1840s character going to a bakery and spending two shillings on a single currant bun.

Of course, it's not always as easy as simply translating figures. Prices of some commodities don't remain fixed, even proportionally fixed. It's all about how easy it is to grow/find/transport/make the item, and how desirable it is, and how much of it can be supplied in a given time.

Think of electronics today. The first primitive PCs in the early 1980s cost a couple of thousand dollars for pitifully low speed and a tiny amount of memory. I spent $1500 on my first (refurbished) desktop computer, which had decent speed and memory for the time, in 1997. In 2009 I spent $300 on my fourth computer, a barely-used refurbished laptop with six times the speed and twenty-five times the memory of my first computer. Today you'll spend about $500 for a brand-new skinny two-pound laptop with twenty times the speed, 150 times more memory, and many, many more features than my first bulky computer had.

Why did the price keep going down while the computers kept getting smaller, faster, and better? Because since the

1980s, computers became steadily cheaper to make. Everybody decided they wanted one; more demand meant more mass production (more availability) which meant less cost per unit; more companies got into the computer-making business and competition and lower manufacturing costs drove prices way, way down, even while the quality grew better and better.

It's the same thing for commodities in past centuries. As mentioned above, you have to be very, very careful about items that we, now, take for granted—and the prices of them. A pound of bread normally cost a somewhat larger percentage of your daily middle-class salary in 1800 than it does now, because farming techniques were not as efficient as today's, but not exorbitantly more—unless the price became a *political* issue, such as when imposed grain taxes and laws about distribution could send prices up nastily, as they often did in pre-revolutionary France. In general, however, wheat is and has been pretty common stuff, except in historic famine years with awful weather and bad harvests. We've been growing it for thousands of years in Europe and Asia and for the past 400 years in North America. Because of industrial farming and storage techniques, wheat  is somewhat easier and cheaper to grow now, and we don't have famine years where the prices shoot up insanely, but the price change over the centuries, when you adjust for inflation, isn't wildly dramatic.

Think about sugar, on the other hand. Where does sugar come from? Not anywhere near most of us in North America or Europe. And in Roman-era, medieval, and Renaissance Europe, honey was the only available local sweetener, while pure sugar—refined from the juice of the sugarcane plant—came from Asia. Sugar had to be imported to Europe by ships (all the way around Africa, remember, from the 1500s until the opening of the Suez Canal in 1870) or on the backs of pack mules or camels, and that meant that sugar was an expensive luxury, just like exotic spices or silk or anything else that was imported from Asia. Really, *really* expensive; only royalty and aristocracy could afford it for their elaborate dishes. In Elizabethan England, a pound of sugar—which isn't a whole lot—cost as much as an entire leg of mutton.

But the price of sugar started going down in the 17th century, when the British and French managed to grow sugarcane plants in their colonies in the Caribbean and established a lot of vast cane plantations. (This, unfortunately, was one of the major reasons the slave trade was such a huge business—thousands of slaves were needed for the brutal sugarcane industry and the labor-intensive processing of cane juice into molasses and sugar.)

Since transporting molasses/sugar across the Atlantic directly to western Europe, or to the North American colonies via the notorious "triangle trade," was still significantly cheaper than transporting sugar around Africa or overland from Asia and paying exorbitant taxes and tolls to every sultan and nawab along the way, the price of sugar soon went down in Europe. It was still expensive; but it was a luxury, like good-quality coffee or imported cheese today, usually within the reach of the average middle-class household, not so *mind-bogglingly* expensive that it was restricted to the super-rich. So while the price of a loaf of bread or a pair of shoes or a horse may have stayed pretty much proportional to income between, say, 1500 and 1800, you can imagine that a pound of sugar cost a much smaller percentage of an average income in London in 1800 than it did in 1400.

The same goes for manufactured goods. Don't assume that the price of a yard of cloth was proportionally the same in 1700 and 1850, after adjusting your prices and coinage to inflation. Because something called the Industrial Revolution happened in between those dates, and the cloth that an English weaver had to make by hand in 1700 from hand-spun thread was being turned out by spinning and weaving machinery at a much, much higher rate in 1850. Suddenly the price dropped and nearly everybody, by the middle of the 19th century, could afford to buy machine-made cloth, instead of spending a lot on handmade cloth from a weaver's workshop or settling for the time- and labor-intensive work of spinning and weaving their own homespun.

So when you're trying to get the prices right, you have to keep in mind what it is you're talking about, and the century or decade you're talking about. Common commodities such as basic foodstuffs cost about the same, percentage-wise, as they do today, but always depending on whether the harvests were good—bad weather and bad harvests, as well as inefficient and outmoded regulations, could make much more of an impact, from time to time, on prices in past centuries than they do today. Imported and manufactured goods, on the other hand, cost a lot (a *lot*) more before the mid 19th century, because shipping foreign goods on smallish sailing ships was a lot more risky and time-consuming and expensive than it is today on giant cargo ships, and because making items by hand took much more time and effort than did mass-producing them by machines in factories.

Just to keep matters interesting, some things cost *less* in previous centuries than they do now—or appeared to. Rent, for example. If you look through someone's diary or accounts or letters from 1750 and find a mention of what the person is paying in rent for his London or Paris apartment per quarter (lodging rent was usually charged in three-month increments), you may think, after calculating what the figure would be equivalent to in 2013 dollars, that rent on an apartment was pretty cheap. Well, it was.

But . . .

Don't forget that what you were renting in 1750 was essentially basic shelter: four walls, a floor, and a ceiling. And glass in the windows if you were lucky.

You were not getting, for your rent, the benefit of running water, water pipes, sewer pipes, electrical wiring, light fixtures, phone lines, gas lines, central heating, a hot water heater, an elevator, a bathroom or toilet, any sort of kitchen or kitchen appliances beyond (maybe) a cooking hearth, or anything else that comes as a matter of course with an apartment in a 21st-century North American building. You weren't even, if you were in a higher income bracket, getting décor: the exquisite carved and painted baroque/rococo panels that décorate formal 17th- or 18th-century rooms were never permanently installed and could be detached from the walls and removed to a new house or apartment whenever the owner desired.

Keep in mind that an average house or apartment house in 1750—or anytime until the late 19th century—was a stone or wood or brick structure and nothing else: no plumbing, no wiring, no heating. And all the money (or time) you spent in carrying or buying water, buying candles, carrying firewood, lighting fires, emptying chamber pots, paying for a bath at the public bathhouse, and doing, or acquiring, or paying servants to do, all the other necessary things that we take for granted as part of our living space and basic services, have to be added to that lowish rent figure. If you add it up, it'll probably come to about the same percentage of your income as your rent does today.

10

Bloopers:
English Aristocratic & Royal Titles

merican writers notoriously and continually get English aristocratic titles wrong and use them improperly, because the rules are so intricate and we don't have a titled aristocracy of our own. But even the British often get English titles wrong.

Even Anne Perry, who should know better, has slipped up about titles now and then in her Victorian mysteries (or an officious copy editor did). In some novels her character Emily's husband, George, is referred to as "Lord Ashworth." In others he's referred to as "Lord George Ashworth." They're *not* the same thing, folks! But Emily, after her marriage, is always referred to in the novels as "Lady Ashworth," not "Lady George Ashworth," and it's a good guess that George was always intended to be a peer in his own right (Viscount Ashworth?) rather than an aristocratic younger son. (The same howler turns up, as it does in many, many other novels and movies, in the 2009 movie *Sherlock Holmes*, in which the villain, Lord Blackwood, is referred to at least once as "Lord Henry Blackwood"—*wrong!*—although the movie is rife with so many other errors and absurdities, including the geographical one of placing Tower Bridge a street or two away from the Houses of Parliament, that we'll just smile politely and ignore everything . . .)

The fiddly hairsplitting rules regarding British titles could fill a fat book, but the distinction between "Lord Ashworth" and "Lord George Ashworth" is the one that nearly everybody gets wrong at one time or another. This error reappears in novel after novel and even in the occasional nonfiction history book, whether about the 17th century or the 20th, so tattoo this on your arm if you have to:

"Lord John Throckmorton"
and
"John, Lord Throckmorton"
DO NOT MEAN THE SAME THING
AND ARE NOT INTERCHANGEABLE.

The basics—I: "Lord John Whatever"

"Lord «Firstname» «Surname»" *is always a younger son of a peer*—**not a peer himself; Lady «Firstname» «Surname»** *is always a peer's daughter*, **but not necessarily a peer's wife.**

"Lord Peter Wimsey"—to use a familiar example from classic mystery fiction—*always* means that Peter is the younger son of a duke or marquess (not earl, baron or viscount) whose *family surname*—**not title**—is Wimsey; "Lady Mary Wimsey" always means that Mary is the daughter of a duke, marquess, or earl (not baron or viscount) whose *family surname* is Wimsey. Fictional sleuth Lord Peter is the younger brother of Gerald, Duke of Denver and was, of course, the second son of the previous duke. Lady Mary Wimsey is Peter and Gerald's sister.

Friends address the duke as "Denver" but Lord Peter as "Lord Peter" (less familiar) or "Wimsey" (more familiar) and Lady Mary as "Lady Mary" unless they're intimate enough to be on a first-name-only basis. Mere acquaintances, of the upper middle class or above, address Lord Peter as "Lord Peter" and his sister as "Lady Mary"; while parlormaids, shopkeepers, garage mechanics, and Peter's devoted man-servant, Bunter, invariably use "my lord/lady" or "your lord/ladyship."

Lord «Firstname» is NEVER addressed or referred to as "Lord «Surname»," which means something else entirely! (A British TV journalist doing a talk with actor Ian Carmichael, who'd played Lord Peter in the 1970s, predictably managed to screw it up and kept referring to "Lord Wimsey" during the interview. I was nearly chewing my fingers off.)

"Lord" or "Lady," when attached to a given name, is a "courtesy title" only, as is the title of a peer's wife ("Lady «Placename»" in social situations), and it can't be passed along to Lord Peter's or Lady Mary's heirs. Even though your fictional Lord Edward McGuffin may be the second son of the eighth Marquess of Throckmorton and the brother of the ninth marquess, Lord Edward's children are always plain Mr. John McGuffin or Miss Lucy McGuffin. This "shutting off" of the honorary titles in succeeding generations is why many of the English upper classes can be closely related to the titled aristocracy but have no titles themselves.

The wife of the younger son of a duke or marquess takes his courtesy title and becomes "Lady «Husband's Firstname» «Husband's Surname»": Lord Peter's wife Harriet (*née* Vane), who began life as a commoner with no title of her own, goes by "Lady Peter Wimsey," NOT "Lady Wimsey" or "Lady Harriet Wimsey." People address her, depending on their social position, as "Lady Peter" (middle class and up) or simply "my lady/your ladyship" (working class).

(If, however, Lord Peter had instead married a hypothetical Lady Priscilla Pygford, the daughter of a duke, marquess, or earl, then Priscilla could have taken her pick of which courtesy title to use and she and her husband, after their marriage, could be Lord and Lady Peter Wimsey—where she takes Peter's courtesy title—*or* Lord Peter and Lady Priscilla Wimsey, where she takes her husband's surname but keeps her own courtesy title.)

~ ~ ~ ~ ~

We know that Lord Peter's sister, Lady Mary Wimsey, marries Peter's friend Detective-Inspector (later Chief Inspector, etc) Parker, a commoner. The issue doesn't come up in the novels, but Mary can choose what to call herself: she can retain her courtesy title at her marriage, if she wishes, and become Lady Mary Parker, *née* Wimsey, rather than Mrs. Charles Parker. At one point Lord Peter suggests that Parker may earn himself a knighthood one day: if that were the case, after Charles is so honored, the couple could choose to be addressed as either "Sir Charles and Lady Parker" (where Mary takes the courtesy title of a knight's wife) *or* "Sir Charles and Lady Mary Parker" (where she retains her own, slightly more prestigious, courtesy title as the daughter of a duke).

If Lord Peter's nephew is killed during World War II, according to some notes that author Dorothy L. Sayers left behind, and Peter's older brother, Gerald, the Duke of Denver, eventually dies without a surviving son to succeed him, then Peter becomes the new Duke of Denver and is no longer called Lord Peter; he's "traded up" his original courtesy title for the much higher-ranking title of duke. (And Harriet, to her great surprise, is no longer Lady Peter Wimsey but the new Duchess of Denver.)

Basically: When you switch titles because of marriage or inheritance, you stick with what you have or you trade up, but never down (unless you happen to vote Labour and detest such relics of feudalism as titles of nobility):

• If a woman with no title marries a title, she takes on the courtesy title attached to it. (Harriet Vane marries Lord Peter Wimsey and becomes Lady Peter Wimsey; your heroine, governess Lucy Jones, marries the Earl of Whitfield and becomes Countess of Whitfield)

• If a woman with a title marries someone with no title, she keeps her own title. (Lady Mary Wimsey marries Charles Parker and becomes Lady Mary Parker—unless she's fiercely determined to be democratic and chooses to be called Mrs. Charles Parker)

• If a woman with a title marries another title of lower or roughly equivalent status, she can choose which to use. (Lady Anne Beech marries Lord William Larch: She can go by Lady Anne Larch or Lady William Larch, whichever she prefers—though if she's a duke's daughter and Lord William is a marquess's son, her rank is a fraction higher than his, which will never, ever matter except in questions of precedence at some insanely formal event like a coronation)

• If a woman with a title marries a higher-ranking title, she "trades up" and goes by the higher-ranking title (Lady Anne Beech marries the Marquess of Frogmore and becomes Marchioness of Frogmore, which has much more clout than mere "Lady Anne").

• **However** (there's always a however): a woman with no title who marries a title (Miss Edna Brown marries Sir Arthur Oakridge and becomes Lady Oakridge; Miss Lucy Jones marries the Earl of Whitfield and becomes Countess of Whitfield), and then gets **divorced** at some point, retains her courtesy title (Lady Oakridge; Countess of Whitfield) **only until she remarries**. Then she loses the courtesy title and takes her new husband's title, whatever it may be—and if he's not titled, she's back to plain "Mrs."

The basics—II: "Lord Whatever"

"Lord «Placename *or* Surname»" refers to a peer—a man who holds a title in his own right. (There are also a very few women who inherit and hold titles in their own right, rather than just marrying them.)

"Lord Denver" means that Lord Peter's brother, Gerald Wimsey, holds a title, is a peer, has a seat in the House of Lords, and probably has a vast estate called Denver on which there is a sprawling Stately Home: he's the Duke of Denver.

(He could also be the Earl of Denver or the Marquess of Denver—but kindly note that Baron, Viscount, and *sometimes* Earl, do not use the pattern of "the [rank] of «Placename»"—a baron or viscount is just "Baron/Viscount «Surname» of «Placename»." Gerald, if he were a viscount rather than a duke, would be Viscount Wimsey of Denver.)

Shakespearian actor Laurence Olivier, to use a real-life example, after he was given a "life peerage" on top of his knighthood, went officially by "Baron Olivier of Brighton,"

or "Lord Olivier"—never "the Baron of Brighton."

"Wimsey," as we know, is Gerald's family name but he is almost never addressed by it; he's called "your/his grace" (very formal), or just "Duke" (less formal) or "Denver" (even less formal) casually among friends who aren't intimate or closely enough related to call him Jerry. "Lord Denver"— "Lord «Placename»"—though strictly accurate, is rarely used when referring to dukes, though "Lord «Placename»" (or "Lord «Surname»," in the case of viscounts and barons and some earls) is correct address for all other ranks of the peerage.

Gerald, as a title holder—the possessor of a dukedom—is NEVER referred to as "Lord Gerald," which is, as we already know, only a courtesy title for younger sons!

A baron or viscount can be referred to, formally, as «Firstname», Lord «Surname» (as in the most familiar example, poet Alfred, Lord Tennyson, formerly Mr. Alfred Tennyson, who was created 1st Baron Tennyson by Queen Victoria—no, "Lord" wasn't his middle name), but this wouldn't be used in ordinary social conversation with him. And only in very formal, ceremonial settings or in official documents is our friend Gerald referred to as "Gerald, Duke of Denver."

When characters are talking about or to your fictional marquess, Lord Throckmorton, and you're dealing with degrees of intimacy and social status in an everyday situation between, say, 1700 and 1950, you can follow these rough guidelines:

• If you're working class or petit-bourgeois—the marquess's butler, or a tenant who rents some of the marquess's property, or the owner of the tobacco shop where the marquess buys his cigars—you'll probably say "His lordship [presuming the other person knows to whom you're referring] asked me the other day . . ." and address him directly as "my lord" or "your lordship" (or use "his/your grace" if he's a duke).

• If you're upper-middle or professional class—the marquess's estate manager or doctor or lawyer—but not a close friend, you'll say "Lord Throckmorton asked me . . ." and address him directly as "my lord" or, more likely, the slightly less deferential "Lord Throckmorton" ("his/your grace" if he's a duke).

• If you're of roughly equal social status—blue-blooded gentry or aristocracy—but barely know the marquess personally, you'll say "Lord Throckmorton asked me . . ." and address him directly as "Lord Throckmorton" (but "your grace" if he's a duke and you're feeling particularly formal; otherwise "Duke" will do). You don't use "my lord" except in highly formal ceremonial occasions, because using "my lord" implies that you're of a lower social level than he, and of course you're not.

• If you're gentry or aristocracy and a friend whom he's known for ten years, but not an intimate friend or close relative on a first-name basis, you'll say "Throckmorton asked me . . ." and also address him directly as "Throckmorton" ("I say, Throckmorton, how about a drink?"). Even if he's a duke.

Why do dukes get the special treatment? It's probably a tradition from the Middle Ages, when dukes were almost always descendants of the royal line somewhere a few generations back, and royal blood . . . got special treatment. **Note:** a "royal duke" today is a member of the royal family, such as the Duke of York (Prince Andrew) or the Duke of Edinburgh (Prince Philip) and is called "His Royal Highness" rather than "His Grace." Prince William's current title, Duke of Cambridge, was granted at the time of his wedding. He'll presumably trade up by the usual rules when Queen Elizabeth dies, Prince Charles becomes king, and William and Kate are eligible to become Prince and Princess of Wales.

Lord Throckmorton's wife is referred to as "Lady Throckmorton" (another courtesy title, conferred by the lady's marital connection to the peer), and she's addressed by social inferiors as "my lady" or "your ladyship" ("your grace" if she's a duchess). An acquaintance of roughly equal social status, if s/he isn't an intimate enough friend or relative to call the lady by her given name, would say either "Lady Throckmorton" (if Lady T is not a duchess) or just "Duchess" if Lady T *is* a duchess.

Let's dissect *Downton Abbey*:

The patriarch, Robert Crawley, is the Earl of Grantham, usually referred to as Lord Grantham (**NOT EVER "Lord Robert,"** and you know why if you've been paying attention). His American-born wife, Cora, is the Countess of Grantham, generally referred to and addressed as Lady Grantham (**NOT EVER "Lady Cora,"** since she wasn't the daughter of an English nobleman).

Their three daughters, however, as daughters of an earl, are Lady Mary Crawley, Lady Edith Crawley, and Lady Sybil Crawley. Lady Sybil, who ran off and married the chauffeur, Tom Branson, if she chose could have been called "Lady Sybil Branson"—though she was so progressive that it looked as if she chose not to use her courtesy title at all, and went by plain "Mrs. Thomas Branson." And since the courtesy titles "shut off" after one generation, their baby daughter Sybbie is Miss Sybil Branson, not "Lady" anything.

Robert's widowed mother (played by Maggie Smith) is the Dowager Countess of Grantham. She's usually referred to as "the Dowager Countess" when necessary, in order to distinguish her from Cora, the current countess (or she can also be referred to as Violet, Countess of Grantham or, less flatteringly, as "old Lady Grantham"—while Cora is always 'the Countess of Grantham" or "Lady Grantham"). She is addressed as "Lady Grantham"/"my lady"/"your ladyship," just as she was when her husband was alive—but *not ever* as "Lady Violet," because even if she had been born Lady Violet Somethingorother, the daughter of a duke, marquess, or earl, she "traded up" her courtesy title for that of countess when she married and became Lady Grantham.[17]

---

[17] A widowed peeress is, however, "the Dowager [title] of «Placename» *only* if the title has passed to a direct male-line descendant of her late husband; in other words, if her son, stepson, or grandson is the new title-holder. If the new lord is her nephew or cousin by marriage, she is not called "Dowager" but simply "Jane, [title] of «Placename»." When Robert dies, Cora, if she's still alive, will NOT be "Dowager Countess," since the new earl will not be a direct descendant in the male line from her hus-

Robert's sister, on the other hand, as the daughter of the previous earl, is Lady Rosamund Painswick (*née* Crawley). She's the widow of a financier who evidently had no title of his own, so she kept her own courtesy title. But if she ever remarried and latched onto someone with an inherited title, she'd take on the courtesy title of a peer's wife and become Viscountess Whatever or Marchioness of Whatever (etc.) and no longer go by "Lady Rosamund."

Since Lord Grantham doesn't have a son, and his first cousin and first cousin once removed went down with the *Titanic*, the new heir to the earldom was his distant cousin, lawyer Matthew Crawley. Matthew, the descendant of a younger son of a previous earl somewhere back a few generations, was plain Mr. Crawley and, since he was the heir to a title but **not** the son of the current holder of the title, he would not have held any titles or courtesy titles of his own until Robert died and Matthew inherited the earldom.

When Matthew and Lady Mary got married, they were officially still Mr. Matthew Crawley and Lady Mary Crawley. If poor Matthew hadn't crashed his roadster and died tragically on the day of his son's birth (how *could* they???), he would have remained Mr. Matthew Crawley until the earl died—then he and Mary would have been the new Earl and Countess of Grantham. Now his unnamed baby son is the heir to the earldom, but *he* won't hold any titles of his own, either, until he inherits the whole kitten—er, that's *the whole kit and caboodle*.

By marrying a distant cousin with the same surname, at least Mary didn't have to order a new set of stationery.

Sometimes all this fiddly detail gets just a little *more* puzzling when a high-ranking English aristocrat's family name is also the name of his title, such as Lord Cornwallis (the guy who lost the Battle of Yorktown in 1781); his full name

---

band—he's Robert's grandson via Mary, but a distant cousin in the male line via Matthew. (I got this one wrong in the first edition of *Underpants*—sorry about that.)

was Charles Cornwallis, Earl (later Marquess) Cornwallis. The Spencers (Princess Diana's[18] family) are also out to confuse you: Di's brother is both Charles Spencer (family name) and the 9th Earl Spencer. If someone is Earl or Marquess «Surname», then, just like barons and viscounts, he doesn't use "of «Surname»"—in other words, Earl Spencer is *not* called "the Earl of Spencer." And neither of these guys, as eldest or only sons, ever goes, or went, by "Lord Charles." (Aren't you glad that the Downton title is "Earl of Grantham" and not the rather silly-sounding "Earl Crawley"?)

Aside: Why, for gosh sakes, are dukes married to duchesses, marquesses to marchionesses, viscounts to viscountesses, barons to baronesses, BUT earls are married to *countesses*???

Blame the Norman Conquest and the effect it had on the English language. Modern English evolved from an amalgamation of Dark Ages Anglo-Saxon (a Germanic language) and  early medieval French. Most of our modern English words for matters related to government, law, aristocracy, and the like are derived from the conquerors' Norman French (except we somehow managed to hold on to both "king" and "queen"— Anglo-Saxon "*cyng*" and "*cwene*"— instead of adopting the French *roi*/*reine* that does linger on in "royal").

Duke, marquess, viscount, and baron are all Anglicizations of French titles (*duc*, *marquis*, *vicomte*, *baron*). "Earl" (*eorl*), the most common pre-Conquest Anglo-Saxon title of nobility, somehow survived intact instead of being translated

---

[18] Yes, I know that Di's formal title was "Diana, Princess of Wales." "Princess Diana" is easier for all of us.

into the French equivalent, *comte*; though the earl's wife, instead of becoming an "earl-ess," eventually became the Anglicized version of the French "*comtesse*."

Honourables, knights, and baronets

Honourables: The sons of earls, viscounts, and barons, and the daughters of viscounts and barons, don't get the courtesy title "Lord/Lady «Firstname»." Instead, they are all "Hons"—on paper known as The Hon. John Smith or The Hon. Elizabeth Brown, although you're not likely to come across the "Honourable" part anywhere in the course of day-to-day life except on an envelope addressed to him or her. If you're referring to, or having a conversation with, a "Hon.", you'd say plain "Mr. Smith" or "Miss Brown."

Knights & Baronets: Knights are given knighthoods as rewards for doing something impressive like curing a disease, being a famous Shakespearean actor, or coping with being Prime Minister. Baronets, on the other hand (the lowest rank of the hereditary, titled aristocracy), inherit their title of "Sir" + «Firstname», but are not considered peers, and do not sit in the House of Lords.

Both knights and baronets are formally announced as Sir «Firstname» «Surname», and are properly called "Sir «Firstname»" by anyone who isn't a close friend. Both knights' and baronets' wives are announced as and addressed as Lady «Husband's Surname». Their servants use the all-purpose "sir" to him, not any form of "my lord"—though they properly address a knight or baronet's wife as "m'lady."

A baronet's full name and title would be, for example (this time borrowing from the Sherlock Holmes canon), "Sir Henry Baskerville of Grimpen, Bt. [or Bart.]." His wife would be "Lady Baskerville." The couple would be announced at a formal function as "Sir Henry and Lady Baskerville" and a knight and his wife would be announced in the same way.

You can tell knights and baronets apart by what comes

after their names: Baronets have "of «Placename»" + "Bt." while knights have an alphabet soup of initials that indicate to which order(s) of chivalry they belong—such as Sir Joseph Porter, K.C.B. ("Knight Commander of the Order of the Bath"), etc.

Sir Henry is *never* called "Sir Baskerville" or "Lord Baskerville" or "Lord Henry" and his wife is *never* "Lady Henry Baskerville" or Lady «Wife's Firstname» (**unless** she was born with a courtesy title of her own).

Now you know enough to keep your basic aristocrats straight, so when you're talking about Reginald, the hunky hero of your romance, who happens to be the Duke of Puddleton, *don't ever* go calling him "Lord Reginald" unless he starts out as Lord Reginald and inherits his dukedom from his older brother in the middle of the story, OK?

More information than you ever wanted to know: The ultimate authority on British titles is Debrett's, which has been following aristocratic family trees for a couple of hundred years. (**www.debretts.com/forms-of-address/titles.aspx**) Their website will give you even more details and tell you just about everything you need to know in order to keep your lords and ladies and their offspring straight, how to address them or refer to them in all sorts of situations, and who's Lord John and who isn't. Another very detailed and useful online resource, specifically geared toward confused writers of HF (particularly Regency romances), is **http://laura. chinet.com/html/titles01.html** .

Keep in mind, however, when referring to Debrett's for your HF, that the rules that the site suggests for such things as directly addressing a peer (simply call him "Lord Throckmorton" in all cases unless he's a duke) are for current 21st-century usage. We're all a bit less formal, and more democratic, these days, even the aristocracy. So while a tailor today would probably address his best customer with "Good morning, Lord Throckmorton," in 1800 or 1900 he would more likely have been a shade more deferential and said "Good morning, my lord."

Regarding royalty

Any movie or book in which somebody addresses an English king before 1534 as "Your Majesty" is probably getting it wrong, and before 1400 is definitely getting it wrong. (The TV miniseries of *The Pillars of the Earth*, set in the 12th century, does this over and over and over again. *The Tudors* has Henry VIII addressed as "Your Majesty" long before 1534, but we might let them get away with that because we know that Henry was just a bit of an egoist.)

The facts: Henry VIII was the first English king to be officially styled "Majesty," after the 1534 Act of Supremacy that declared Henry supreme head of the Church in England and equal in earthly status to an emperor (the Holy Roman Emperor was styled "Majesty"). Before Henry VIII, English kings were addressed as "Sire" or "Your Grace" and referred to as "His Grace," though 15th-century kings were called "Majesty" from time to time in official proclamations and so on. But if your novel is set before 1400, always stick with "Sire" or "Your Grace" when someone is talking to the king.

Regarding numbers: A reigning monarch (or pope) whose name hasn't been used by a previous monarch in his/her own country goes by King (or Queen or Pope) «Firstname», period. *Not* King/Queen «Firstname» the First. And s/he goes by King/Queen «Firstname», **without a number**, all his/her life and in the archives and the history books for however many years or centuries after his/her death until a second «Firstname» takes the throne.[19]

---

[19] This applies right now to our new pope, Pope Francis—he should *not* be called Pope Francis I, ever, until the future date when there's a Pope Francis II.

They don't refer to King John as King John I or Queen Victoria as Queen Victoria I. So since Elizabeth II is a few centuries still in the future of your 16th-century story, please, *pleeeeze* don't have Sir Francis Drake or Will Shakespeare talk about "our good Queen Elizabeth the First"—or, for that matter, have someone in 1853 mention something that took place "back in the days of Elizabeth the First," when he should be saying merely, "back in the days of Queen Elizabeth."

And then there's this one. Anyone who has been studying history for a while and commits this ought to be thoroughly ashamed of him/herself, but it does rear its hideously ugly head now and then, so:

Monarchs (and popes and other folks with an attached number in Roman numerals) are NOT referred to, on the page, as "Henry **the** VIII" or "Pope John **the** XXIII."

Yank that "the" out, smack it down, and stamp on it. Hard.

When speaking, we *say* "Louis the Fourteenth" or "Pope Clement the Fifth"; it's usually written out this way only within spoken, quoted dialogue, and it's optional. *The Daughter of Time*, which provides the following example, is a little inconsistent with this, but it never uses the horrid and erroneous "Henry the VIII" or "Richard the III":

> Grant … was half asleep, when a voice in his mind said: "But Thomas More was Henry the Eighth."
>
> This brought him wide awake. … What the voice had meant, of course, was not that Thomas More and Henry the Eighth were one and the same person, but that … Thomas More belonged to the reign of Henry the Eighth.
>
> … If Thomas More was Henry VIII's Chancellor, then he must have lived through the whole of Henry VII's long reign as well as Richard III's. There was something wrong somewhere.

It's a convention that **the "the" is implied and not included** when writing down the name and Roman numeral of a monarch—or indeed, anyone else with a Roman numeral after his or her name, even Thurston Howell III. *Not* "Thurston Howell **the** III."

When writing it, it's just King (or Queen or Prince or Emperor or Pope) «Firstname» «Roman Numeral»: "King George V"; "Catherine II"; "Pope Clement VI"; "Louis XIV"; and for the rest of us (adding a surname, of course), "Mr. Frederick Scroggins IV." Period.

Commit this to memory and tell everyone you know, because if I can come across "King Henry the VIII" (shudder) in an otherwise intelligent and literate professional book review at *Publishers Weekly*, of all things, then the world of words is in a sorry state.

11

Bloopers: Lights Out!

ne of the biggest misconceptions about the past that historical movies have to answer for is the astonishing amount of light that always seems to be available. Nighttime scenes in movies are always wonderfully well-lit by a few candles or torches, maybe with a little help from a moon that is always conveniently full at the right time.

Sadly, it's unavoidable from a technical point of view, because of the limitations of film: you can't film a nighttime scene lit only by normal candle- or torchlight and expect it to be watchable. One very rare exception to this is Stanley Kubrick's *Barry Lyndon* (1975), for which Kubrick actually did light some indoor sets with genuine candlelight and used a high-tech, extremely fast film in order to make the scenes viewable. But watch *Barry Lyndon* sometime and see just how many candles he had to use, in order to get what is still fairly dim lighting.

The facts: for most of human history, people—except for the very richest—got up at dawn, with the daylight, and went to bed at dusk, when the light failed. If they stayed up any later, as they might have on a winter's night when the days were short, they were probably clustered around the cooking/

heating fire. This type of fire (in the *middle* of the room or hut or great hall in the castle, beneath a hole in the roof, until the 1300s—chimneys hadn't been invented yet) provided just enough light for Og the Cro-Magnon or Dafydd the Dark Ages Welsh peasant or Johann the medieval German shoemaker to tell who was sitting opposite him, and to grope his way out of the cave/room/hut to take a leak without tripping over something. Hence the popularity of the medieval tavern and the seventeenth-century coffeehouse: for the price of a tankard of ale or a demitasse of black coffee, you got the companionship of your neighbors plus free heat and light for a few hours during long, dark, cold winter nights.

Fire, by the way, before the self-igniting match was invented in the early 19th century (see below), isn't nearly as easy to make as many historical movies and novels would have us believe. If your kitchen fire went out, it was much easier to run over to your next door neighbor and ask for a hot coal or two than to labor for ten minutes hunched over your flint and tinder, trying to coax a spark into life.

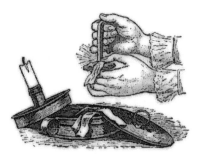

The first friction matches (which were lit by running the tip of the match through sandpaper) appeared in 1826; Lucifer matches were sold in London beginning in 1829; phosphorus matches (instead of sulfur) were available beginning in 1839; and safety matches appeared in 1855.

Until the late 19th century, artificial light was difficult to maintain and therefore expensive. When, like light from ancient oil lamps that were little more than wicks sticking out of little clay dishes, it *wasn't* expensive, it was smelly, smoky, sooty, and usually wildly inadequate. What's more, since all artificial light came from open flames of some sort, whether fireplaces, torches, candles, stinky oil lamps, or far less stinky 19th-century whale oil or kerosene lamps, it wasn't particularly safe. (The trendy custom of the Christmas tree—introduced to Queen Victoria's England by her German husband, Prince Albert—probably was responsible for more disastrous house fires in 19th-century England and North America than any other single cause, because Victorian Christmas trees were lit with small candles and the effect, though beautiful, was horrendously dangerous. Combine a few dozen burning candles, a drying-out pine tree, a lot of heavy Victorian curtains, tablecloths, and other assorted draperies, and a clumsy passerby, and . . . oops.)

Streets, meanwhile, until the 19th century, were barely lit with candle lanterns or primitive oil lamps, or not lit at all, though it's easy to forget this with the ever-present electric "light pollution" of the 20th and 21st centuries making all our cities and towns navigable at any time of the night. Preindustrial city streets, most of which were narrow and twisty, shutting out any light that might have crept in from a window, overhead lantern, or full moon, were usually pitch-dark and dangerous, sheltering countless pickpockets and muggers in their deep shadows.

So try to forget every movie you've ever seen in which a nighttime room or street is beautifully lit by a couple of candelabra or lanterns, and think about light. Try to remember the darkest unlit back country road or hiking trail you've ever walked or driven down at midnight, and now imagine that same path or road lined with four-story buildings, with very little light escaping through the tightly-closed shutters over the windows. That'll give you some idea of the darkness of the average city street at any time before the 19th century, whether 2nd-century Rome or 16th-century London.

Of course, it would have been less dark indoors, but:

Turn off all the lights in a room at night and pull the curtains (thick ones) against any street lights or light from your neighbors' windows. Now light a couple of candles.

Romantic?

Well, maybe.

It's also a lousy light for *doing* anything, particularly reading, unless you have about ten candles burning at once in your candelabrum. Light from a single candle is good for practically nothing except for lighting yourself up to bed without tripping and falling down stairs.

And candles, like any other manufactured item in the centuries before mass production, took a lot of time and effort to make and therefore took up a good part of one's household budget. (If you were urban, you didn't make them for yourself if you could avoid it; rendering fat and butcher's scraps and roadkill for tallow is one of the more smelly and disgusting jobs that people gladly handed over to manufacturers, even before mechanization.) What's more, tallow candles, the cheaper option, stink (like hot rancid pig fat), gutter, and sputter. Beeswax candles, which burn more evenly and smell much nicer, cost quite a lot more and were a luxury for the comfortable middle class and above.

One of the biggest everyday expenses for a grand aristocratic or royal household in the 17th and 18th century, in fact, must have been candles. Those enormous crystal chandeliers in the great palaces of the time held twenty to fifty candles each—a large ballroom would have had anywhere from six to twelve chandeliers—and if a ball went on long enough, the candles would have to be replenished while the guests were at supper (in a nearby room where there were also a few hundred candles burning). In 18th-century France, candles, especially the best-quality beeswax candles from Trudon, candle-makers to the king, which were *de rigueur* for churches and aristocratic households, cost so much that some courtiers at Versailles actually made a nice little side income by collecting and selling half-burned candles from the palace. (Re-lighting a half-used candle was considered highly inappropriate for royalty, who had to have the best and most perfect of everything; just as they couldn't possibly eat anything but an untouched dish, etiquette decreed that the royals had to start with pristine, unburned candles in any room they entered.)

Keep in mind that every nighttime scene in your historical novel, both inside and outside, would have been a lot darker than you can't help imagining it—and lighting that dark space would have cost an awful lot of time or money.

12

Bloopers:
A Quick Chapter On Slooooow Travel

n an age of hybrid cars, high-speed trains, jet planes, and space shuttles, it's easy to forget that, until less than two centuries ago, the fastest anyone had ever traveled on land was at the speed of a galloping horse—about 25 miles per hour. (Horizontally traveled, at least; we're not counting the speed you might have reached if you'd fallen into the Grand Canyon.) Before you send someone from Philadelphia to Boston in two days in 1775, think again about the difficulties and discomforts of preindustrial travel.

Travel on land was *slow*. The Romans laid down an incredible network of roads throughout their empire, but they remained the state of the art for the next two thousand years, and when the empire disintegrated, road maintenance ceased to be a priority in many areas. Towns of any size had at least a few cobbled streets by the late Middle Ages, simply for the sake of keeping the traffic moving on major arteries, but—until the 19th century—where no ancient Roman roads existed, the roads between villages, towns, and/or cities were not paved or even cobbled; they were, at best, well-maintained dirt and gravel wagon tracks.

Most ordinary people, especially city folk, could not afford to own and maintain a horse and conveyance of their own; when they wanted to travel between cities, public transportation or hiring horses was the way to go. (The well-off rode inside the coach; poorer people sat outside, on top, with the baggage, and coped with the weather.) The 18th- or 19th-century stagecoach, pulled by four or six horses, went between four and seven miles per hour if the weather was good and the road was in decent repair and non-muddy, which it usually wasn't except in midsummer. This meant that, with meal breaks and the short breaks required every ten miles or so to change horses, an average long day's coach travel covered between 60 and 100 miles. The traveler from Philadelphia probably made it to Boston (about 300 miles away) in a coach in about a week, if he was lucky with weather and road conditions.

Riders on horseback could go faster than carriages could, but with less comfort. Horses are strong and fast, but they can't keep up a 25-mile-per-hour gallop for long, and need to be exchanged frequently for fresh mounts; no one who wanted to get somewhere—without killing his horse—would have gone at racing speed for any extended length of time.

If you wanted to get somewhere quickly and didn't have access to a string of fresh saddle horses along the way, in France, for example, the very fastest early 19th-century express mail van, a light covered wagon pulled by three horses, could make an average eight miles per hour. Traveling continuously overnight, with quick stops for changing horses and dropping off the mail bundles, it could cover 250 miles in about 30 hours—but only someone in a desperate hurry and indifferent to acute discomfort would have considered taking the single passenger seat on one of them.

~ ~ ~ ~ ~

If roads in the Early Modern era (16th, 17th and 18th centuries) were bad, medieval roads were worse. Medieval roads between town and town were little more than muddy trails, and usually went through dense forests infested with bandits. It probably took at least a week to ten days on horseback to travel the 200 miles between London and York—more time if traveling when the days were shorter and sunset fell earlier, for no one wanted to be on the road after dark.

Since medieval roads were so bad, carriage or wagon travel was rare; most people traveled on horseback—or simply walked. A specific type of horse, the palfrey, was bred for carrying well-off travelers. Palfreys are trained to use a particular gait, called an "amble" (sort of like "power walking" for horses) which is faster than a walk and, while slower than trotting, is much smoother than a trot or canter, which is a major consideration for your backside if you're going to be straddling a horse for the next six days.

Traveling by **ship** was a little less uncomfortable (unless you had a major problem with seasickness) and a little faster, but not by much. Anyone crossing the Atlantic Ocean from Europe to New England in a sailing ship before 1830 or so expected the journey to take between four and six weeks—eight if he was unlucky. No one crossed the Atlantic any faster than that until the mid 19th century, the age of the steamship, when the crossing eventually speeded up to about two weeks by the 1870s. The great passenger liners such as *Titanic* and her sisters finally trimmed the crossing to about a week in the early 20th century.

A traveler going by boat on a river might go at a decent speed downstream—up to ten miles per hour—but the return journey would probably take at least twice as long, if they had to sail or row upstream against the current. In 1807, the first commercial steamboat, Robert Fulton's North River Steamboat (later the *Clermont*), while far more comfortable and reliable than a sailing ship or a stagecoach, still took 32 hours to

the "Clermont"

complete the 150-mile trip upstream on the Hudson River between New York City and Albany—a land speed of about 4.5 miles per hour.

The mid 18th century in England and the 1810s and 1820s in the northeastern United States saw the advent of commercial canals—the superhighways of their day. If traveling by canal boat was no faster than coach travel (canal boats were towed by horses or mules), at least it was far smoother, quieter, more spacious, and more comfortable for passengers. Canal boats, moreover, could carry large amounts of freight with very little effort; one or two mules could tow a heavily laden boat with ease along a currentless, obstacle-free canal.

The railroads, the great transportation breakthrough of the Industrial Revolution, at last eclipsed the canals by the middle of the 19th century. Railroads began in the 1820s as large horse-drawn carriages on rails (see illustration), which could travel faster and more smoothly than on muddy, rutted, pot-holed early-19th-century roads. The steam locomotive speed-ed things up considerably. "Stephenson's Rocket," the first ef-fective locomotive, built in England in 1829, had a top speed (terrifying for the time) of just 28 miles per hour (45 km/h), though the speed of locomotives improved quickly over the next couple of decades. But even Stephenson's Rocket went four times as fast as the average stagecoach on a good day.

BALTIMORE AND OHIO RAILROAD, 1830.

Basic Rules
You Need To Keep In Mind
That Will Help You Avoid
the Silly Mistakes

General Rule
No. 4

Don't Just Swallow the Propaganda, Clichés, & Myths

In other words: Just because a hostile or worshipping historian (or novelist), twenty or fifty or two hundred years after the fact, made a certain eye-popping claim about an event or person or issue, that doesn't necessarily make his claim accurate.

The propaganda, intentional or not, of later decades/centuries/eras can give us false impressions of almost anything, from the trivial (the myth that nobody between the fall of Rome and the 19th century ever bathed—see the next chapter) to the massively significant (misrepresenting entire historical events). The established clichés about an issue, event, or era have usually evolved from that propaganda. Opinions and strong feelings run deep about controversial periods of history, usually ones that involve clashing political or religious ideologies, and can taint or distort interpretations in all kinds of ways.

To use just one particular example with which I'm extremely familiar, the French Revolution is still, after 200-plus years, a very divisive subject among some people (mostly right-wingers, professional historians, and the French). Thousands of books have been written about it, many of which claim it was a terrible, horrible, icky event in every possible way and the precursor of modern totalitarianism, as if Hitler and Stalin couldn't have come up with the idea of massacring millions without the Revolution's (far tinier, numerically speaking) example showing them the way. And many others argue that it was—despite its violence—inevitable and necessary in its legal reforms, which dragged the most powerful and influential kingdom in Europe out of the remnants of medieval feudalism and into the modern Western world.

And the totally predictable, clichéd falsehood I see in at least three-quarters of all works of HF written in English and set in this period is the gratuitous, over-the-top exaggeration of the "horrors" of the Revolution. These hysterical, way-out-of-proportion depictions appear in everything from *A Tale of Two Cities*, the Top Literary Classic, to the witless romantic fluff of the Pimpernel novels. And then there's a recently published atrocity that I sampled not long ago (with shudders and unable to get past the first pages), whose author had apparently done no other historical research than watch a bad movie of *The Scarlet Pimpernel* and seems to be firmly convinced . . . no need to look up pointless things like *facts* . . . that even Nazism couldn't match the evil, evil, evil French Revolution in sheer bloodshed.

In all these novels and many others, the Revolution is reduced to the Terror and only the Terror, and Paris is invariably a slaughterhouse: everybody is in constant fear and up to their ankles in blood; thousands of innocent, innocent nobles (because none of them were *ever* the selfish, arrogant, conniving, corrupt, royal-arse-kissing nobles, of course) are always trying to flee the city; said irreproachable nobles are constantly being captured by viciously cackling peasants (who are always knitting when they're not viciously cackling) and immediately packed off to the guillotine, which is chopping off at least a hundred blameless heads a day for a couple of years, morning till night. (There are about nine major historical howlers in that sentence. Yes, the French Revolution was a bloody affair. But it wasn't *nearly* as bloody as Victorian novelists, with their disproportionate fixation on the Terror in Paris, *assumed* it was—and obviously many modern novelists have, too, after watching too many inept film versions of *A Tale of Two Cities* [*Do not borrow your period information from other people's historical novels or movies*].)

And why did Victorian novelists *assume* all this? Because they used, for their background research, a lot of early-19th-century histories and memoirs of the Revolution, and believed everything in them. (It's a history book, so it must be right, right?)

But most of the histories were written by conservative, Francophobic English historians. And most of the memoirs were written by émigré French aristocrats (usually hard-line royalists who'd been abruptly deprived, poor things, of their unearned class privileges) who had an axe to grind because they'd hated every single thing about the Revolution from the beginning—long before the Terror—even while the rest of

James Gillray, "*Un petit Souper à la Parisienne*, or, a Family of Sans Culotts refreshing after the fatigues of the day" (1792). British anti-French propaganda caricaturing Parisians as grotesque cannibals.

the population of France had been delighted by the reforms it brought about. These émigrés, a.k.a. the 18th-century One Percent, had usually lost all their wealth when they had fled France and were understandably bitter; but if you don't take that furious bitterness (and their passionate, narrow-minded, and often self-interested devotion to the dysfunctional, clueless French monarchy and decadently corrupt court) into account when you read their memoirs, you're going to get a very skewed idea of the French Revolution.

The trouble with buying unquestioningly into 19th-century English histories of the Revolution, meanwhile, is that the English and the French have had a long, long history of officially hating each other, from the Middle Ages right up until the Battle of Waterloo. Many 19th-century English historians were ready to believe any kind of lurid account that made the French and their revolution look bad, because they'd all grown up hearing from their nannies that "Boney [Napoleon] would get them if they weren't good" and hearing from their parents and schoolmasters that everything about those nasty French revolutionaries—who had overthrown their king and queen and, what's more, *insulted* them before chopping their heads off—was to be looked upon with horror, fear, and disgust. And since the French were traditional enemies of the English to begin with, it wasn't hard to think the worst of everything about the Revolution ("such a disgraceful event wouldn't happen *here*—we're English!"[20]).

Anything you read about some event of the French Revolution that's particularly bloodcurdling—if it was set down by a rabidly royalist French aristocrat or a conservative 19th-

---

[20] The British, throughout the French Revolution, always seemed to have a sort of amnesia about chopping their own king's head off 144 years previously. They may, at the time, have subconsciously concluded that the disrespectful—though not at all physically cruel—way in which the French king and queen were regarded and treated during their imprisonment made all the difference between the "legal" English execution of Charles I and the "massacres" of Louis XVI and Marie-Antoinette.

century Englishman (or even American)—needs to be looked into further before you swallow it whole. Postrevolutionary Anglo-Saxon historians were willingly buying into the anti-French and anti-revolutionary propaganda of their own time and of past centuries, and we, the writers of HF, have to be very careful about how we buy into *their* swallowed, digested, and regurgitated propaganda.

I found a blatant example of an opposing viewpoint gratuitously distorting a historical work quite recently, in *Madame Roland*, a biography of French Revolutionary figure Marie-Jeanne Roland (1754-1793), originally published by American author and pop historian John S. C. Abbott in 1850. It's clear, right from the beginning, that Abbott detests the Revolution but adores his subject. The book is much too tedious, hero-worshipping, amateurishly error-ridden, and generally Victorian to discuss at length, but when Madame Roland is condemned to death, the author writes:

> The morning of the 10th of November, 1793, dawned gloomily upon Paris. It was one of the darkest days of that reign of terror which, for so long a period, enveloped France in its somber shades. The ponderous gates of the courtyard of the Conciergerie opened that morning to a long procession of carts loaded with victims for the guillotine. ... The last cart was assigned to Madame Roland . . .
>
> ... The long procession arrived at the guillotine, and the bloody work commenced. The victims were dragged from the carts, and the ax rose and fell with unceasing rapidity. Head after head fell into the basket, and the pile of bleeding trunks rapidly increased in size.

(The stirringly melodramatic phrase "the Reign of Terror," by the way, was invented and popularized not by the French, who never used anything but "La Terreur" during the Revolution, but by—surprise!—Abbott's fellow 19th-century English-speaking historians.)

So after we quickly pass over the fact that Abbott got the

date wrong—November 8th, not 10th—and ignore the over-the-top, novelistic writing in what is supposed to be nonfic-tion, what we need to look at again is these straightforward, categorical statements of Abbott's, describing an image oh-so-familiar from two centuries of pop fiction:

> … A long procession of carts loaded with victims for the guillotine. … Head after head fell into the basket, and the pile of bleeding trunks rapidly increased in size.

Vivid, yes?

But the "long procession of carts loaded with victims" and "the pile of bleeding trunks" that he describes so juicily and hand-wringingly, and which promptly recall blood-and-thunder scenes from *The Scarlet Pimpernel*, are entirely Ab-bott's invention. Made up out of whole cloth and unblush-ingly presented to us as factual "history" in his history book.

The way he tells it?

It. Didn't. Happen.

It's too bad Mr. Abbott hadn't been able, before he wrote his book, to visit Paris and look at the archives of the Revo-lutionary Tribunal (which was responsible for all the official death sentences of the Terror in Paris), or at a Parisian news-paper from November 1793—in other words, to research pri-mary sources for his facts, rather than let his imagination run wild, influenced by hostile propaganda that he'd absorbed from other people's histories. Because if he had, he would have soon found out that the total number of people guillotined in Paris on November 8th, 1793—including Madame Roland her-self—was . . . two.

The average number of people guillotined per day in Paris in all of September, October, November, and December 1793, during the first several months of the Terror, was . . . two.[21]

Not a hundred per day, not fifty or sixty, not even a couple

---

[21] Wallon, Henri, *Histoire du Tribunal Révolutionnaire de Paris* [vol. 2]. Paris: Hachette, 1880. Wallon's in-depth and definitive six-volume, 3,000-page scholarly study is based directly on the Tribunal's records.

of dozen, any of which is pretty clearly what Abbott had in mind when he started describing "the darkest days of that reign of terror" and implying that this sort of thing had already been going on on a daily basis for months (or maybe years).

Two.

(No, an average of two executions a day, every day, is still not something we really want to see. But it doesn't come remotely close to Abbott's lurid fantasy of "a long procession of carts loaded with victims.")

So here's Mr. Abbott, doing his second-hand research with his limited 19th-century American resources, and buying into the shocked—*shocked* I say!—respectability of the Anglo-Saxon party line of the postrevolutionary era (*"That horrible French Revolution was totally evil evil evil because they dared to abolish their monarchy, and surely those wicked Frenchies killed off half the population of France!"*). And so he doesn't bother to look up hard numbers, even if he ever had access to them. And he goes on to *assume*, and suggest to us, that dozens or hundreds of lily-white innocents must have been guillotined *every single day* in Paris throughout the entire fourteen-month Terror—rather than the far, far smaller actual numbers, whose ranks included a significant proportion of the sort of sleazy profiteers, troublemakers, military deserters, and petty crooks whom any late-18th-century British court, in the normal course of business, would have sentenced to hanging in a heartbeat.

So Abbott plunks down his shameless bit of hyperbole as if it were absolute fact—*"what the heck, eh? So-and-So's history suggests hundreds of victims a day—let's stick it to those godless Frogs!"* And this Big Fat Falsehood presented to us in an ostensible work of nonfiction, like many similar tall tales, finds its way into the overwrought historical novels and becomes just one more lie reinforcing already-common misconceptions that distort the image of an entire event and era.

(It's a history book, so it must be right, right?)

OK. This chapter isn't actually intended as a lecture on the French Revolution, but all of the preceding is just an example of how even "professional" historians and chroniclers can exaggerate or falsify the "facts," whether intentionally or not. The same warning goes for any controversial period—revolutions, conquests (regime changes), and religious upheavals providing the most divisive issues: You should probably be very cautious before, say, blindly accepting early Christian accounts of Rome in the second century A.D. Or hostile second-century Roman accounts of early Christians and other wacky cults.

"Truth isn't in accounts but in account books." (*The Daughter of Time*)

Josephine Tey's *The Daughter of Time* (1951), one of the best mystery novels ever written, examines the reputation of England's last Plantagenet monarch, Richard III, from the point of view of the mid 20th century. It provides a brilliant example of how historical facts can be deliberately distorted and covered up by "the winners" of a military conquest and change of dynasty, in order to make the previous regime look bad, and how that misinformation ends up in all the history books (secondary sources)—and also how pieces of the truth, which can be reassembled like a jigsaw puzzle to come up with a different picture, can lie in ignored archives (primary sources: basic facts of dates, laws, and public records).

While Richard III was undoubtedly no saint, this novel has opened a couple of generations' worth of readers' eyes to the likelihood that—despite anti-Richard, pro-Tudor propaganda like Shakespeare's play *King Richard III* and countless later histories that uncritically toed the party line—he was no blindly malignant, bloodily ruthless, psychopathic monster either. (Nor was he the misshapen hunchback whom Shakespeare so colorfully describes. The famous recent discovery and authentication of Richard's skeleton—"the king in the car park"—have proved conclusively that he had pronounced scoliosis, a *sideways* curvature of the spine, which, in life, would have given him one shoulder slightly higher than the other, but nothing more.)

Early Tudor chroniclers gave Richard, after his death, very bad press, which was enthusiastically augmented in the following centuries by such entertaining—but wildly inaccurate— portrayals like Shakespeare's, which is really just one step short of mustache-twirling melodrama, with Richard as Snidely Whiplash. Did Richard III really murder his nephews? Probably not, when a little research among primary sources shows us there were a couple of other candidates with much better motives to do so. But the anti-Richard historical propaganda persists.

Keep an open mind before unquestioningly believing Catholic accounts of the English Reformation, or English Protestant accounts of the 16th-century Catholic Church. Read a contemporary Catholic depiction of Anne Boleyn and she's a whore, a witch, and a bitch; while a Protestant depiction (particularly one written fifty or sixty years later by people who wanted to suck up to Elizabeth I, her daughter—there's a prize example in Shakespeare's *King Henry VIII*) will convince you that Anne was an angelic vision of purity and a saintly martyr of the English Reformation. But the truth, you can be sure, was somewhere in the middle.

The short version of all of this is that the researcher has to keep in mind, at all times, that chroniclers have a point to make and a point of view to put across. And—particularly in previous centuries, before professional historians decided they should be as impartial as possible (though not all have agreed to that, even now)—they were just as eager to make their enemies look bad as they were to make their own side look good. Keep an open mind, always remember whose account you're reading and what his biases may be, and focus on verifiable facts, ideally from primary sources like records, archives, and (neutral) eyewitness accounts, rather than just on opinions.

In other words . . .

Never assume.

13

Bloopers:
Hygiene, Cleanliness, & More

ersonal cleanliness, or the lack of it, in past centuries is an issue which, paradoxically, careless authors of HF can get wrong by buying into the prevailing myth and trying too hard to get it right.

We've all seen the movies: filmmakers from the 1970s, scoffing at cheesy old Hollywood movies of King Arthur or Robin Hood where everything looks like an improbably perfect and squeaky-clean movie set of an almost Disneyfied medieval fantasyland, tried to go in the other direction and made their period films as raw and "realistic" as possible. So they filmed on location at genuine half-ruined castles that, in truth, didn't look the least bit as new and un-grungy as they really would have looked seven hundred years before. (A genuine medieval castle in the fourteenth century, while it wouldn't have been as spiffy as the *Robin Hood* sets on the MGM back lot, would never have had interior walls of bare, grim, gray stone, at least in the lord's quarters and the major public areas—they were plastered over, and brightly painted where they weren't covered with brightly colored tapestries.)

The "realistic" moviemakers emphasized the nastiness of

everyday life in past centuries—especially the Middle Ages—with lots of mud and horse manure everywhere, chickens flapping in the street, a few rats, and filthy, lice-ridden peasants with warts and sores and revolting diseases, while the grimy lords in their cold, drafty castles were scarcely better, flinging bones over their shoulders to the dogs that fought for the scraps in the layers of dirty rushes. The "Bring out your dead!" and "Communist Peasants" scenes and others from *Monty Python and the Holy Grail* are an excellent sendup of all these movies, with "gritty realism" brought to an over-the-top level of filth, yuckiness, and lack of personal hygiene for everyone.

The truth is, through most of human history, everybody who *wanted* to be clean—and who was able to be or could afford to be clean—*was* clean. Og the Cro-Magnon may not have smelled very good during the long Ice Age winters, but it's likely that as soon as he could stand the icy river in spring, he stepped into it and scrubbed himself off.

The practical limitations on cleanliness are mostly about how difficult and/or expensive it is to keep oneself clean. To have a real bath in the Middle Ages, you had to get your (wooden) tub, lug it to the room with the fireplace, line the tub with sheets (you don't want splinters in your backside), lug in many bucketfuls of water, heat the water over the fire, fill the tub . . . and then empty the tub afterward. But a medieval noble, who had plenty of servants to carry tubs and water, and plenty of firewood with which to heat the water, probably had a bath whenever he or she wanted one.

What's more, we have to remember that there's no particular difference, in the final result, between bathing (immersing yourself in a tub) and washing (sponging yourself well with a few quarts of water and a little soap). Our medieval lord or lady probably had at least a good "basin wash" or sponge bath every day—we who enjoy our daily showers tend to forget that a gallon of warm water in the sink can get us just as clean as a shower can. (If your hot-water heater dies on you over Thanksgiving weekend, you'll soon discover the virtues of an electric kettle and a stoppered sink.) Medieval books of

household management usually include plenty of recipes for making soap, and not just harsh laundry soap, but nicely scented varieties—obviously people were using it on their persons.

No doubt the peasants living on our medieval noble's estate weren't nearly as clean as their lord and lady were, since firewood (or peat or dried cow pies) had to be laboriously gathered and were more valuable for cooking and heating than for a luxury like washing the body, but anyone who lived near a stream, river, or lake must have bathed in it during the summer. The urban poor, living in crowded, dirty conditions and with less access to open water unless they went to the banks of the filthy river, were probably the least likely to be clean.

But why do we have this persistent image of *all* Europeans in the past, from the fall of Rome to at least the 18th century—including the wealthy and the royals, who could well afford hot baths and soap whenever they wished—being filthy, smelly, and unhygienic?

The truth is, the "smelly wealthy European" image dates from about the 16th-17th centuries rather than from the Middle Ages, and it was largely a consequence of both the fabulous clothing of the rich and a firm belief in what we'd call today "junk science."

The Romans, we know, were obsessively clean and built aqueducts and public baths everywhere they settled. When the Roman Empire collapsed and the Dark Ages (roughly A.D. 450-800) took over western Europe, personal hygiene was one of the things that fell somewhat by the wayside, partly because it was less practical in the rougher, unstable society of the post-Roman era (and the baths and aqueducts had been damaged or destroyed), and partly because the early Christians had no use for bodily cleanliness, for several reasons. Bathing, in the Dark Ages, was too closely linked in people's memories with that decadent pagan Roman society that had once persecuted good Christians; fanatical Christians believed that dirt and illness, like everything else, were all God's creations, and those who impiously tried to remove the grime that had collected on their bodies (let alone practiced medicine!) were therefore deliberately going against God's will; and they also believed that "mortification of the body"—denying oneself fleshly pleasures like cleanliness and smelling nice—was good for the soul. Obviously the expression "Cleanliness is next to godliness" hadn't come into circulation yet,[22] and undoubtedly there were some pretty fragrant characters—especially "holy men"—going about during the European Dark Ages.

After a couple of hundred years, though, as medieval technology improved and society grew stronger and more stable, bathing came back into fashion—it's likely that everybody who wasn't blindly obeying the dubious doctrine that dirt and b.o. were part of God's plan, and who could afford sufficient hot water to keep clean, tried his best to keep clean. Medieval people of the middle and upper classes were clean enough (*someone* used that scented soap), even if their towns weren't. The Middle Ages, however, have had bad press from Renaissance chroniclers, who were eager to emphasize how much more

---

[22] Various sources claim it's a Hebrew proverb from the writings of a 2nd-century A.D. rabbi, but the earliest record of it in English seems to be in Francis Bacon's "Advancement of Learning" (1605).

learned and civilized than their forebears they were. So Renaissance historians didn't have much good to say about customs of a few hundred years before, and rarely mentioned that their great-great-grandfathers frequently washed.

Conversely, the Renaissance learning that was the basis of a lot of our modern science also was responsible for some big fat scientific fallacies of the time. And one of these was Renaissance and Early Modern medicine and its theories of disease; Western medicine, which had been remarkably advanced in the ancient world, had never really recovered from the massive setbacks of the Dark Ages and was a mishmash of incomplete classical texts, Arab texts smuggled in from the Middle East, ancient folk healing, and sheer superstition.

No one knew how and why contagious diseases were transmitted. So when "science" finally progressed past the dogma that diseases were invariably a punishment from God, the most convincing theory (until late-19th-century doctors finally turned for good to the real culprits—germs) was that disease was caused by "miasma," or bad air, brought on by the filth and crowding (and manure piles) of large towns or, in the countryside, smelly swamps or wetlands (or manure piles). This theory had been popular since ancient times, and certainly there was a lot of stinky air around in a typical Renaissance city with its practically nonexistent sanitation, especially in poor quarters.

How did you catch diseases from bad air? By breathing it, of course, but evidently—according to 16th- and 17th-century doctors—you could also absorb the bad air through your skin, via your pores. And so Renaissance physicians concluded that the more open one's pores were, the more likely they were to absorb infections from that bad air. Thus, open pores = bad and closed pores = good.

Now anybody who's taken a really hot shower can see that our pores open with moist heat (bathing, steam baths, etc.) and close almost to invisibility when we're cool and dry. So the physicians concluded that the simplest way to avoid absorbing diseases through the skin was to keep the pores as closed as possible. Washing the body opens the pores; therefore any kind of bathing or cleaning oneself, especially with warm water, was highly dangerous. In fact, a good layer of dried sweat and everyday grime would help seal those pores and serve as a protective armor for the skin. Keep those pores tightly closed at all times by never, ever washing your body!

Not everybody followed this line of thinking. Henry VIII, for one, had elaborate bathing rooms in all his palaces and frequently bathed. Elizabeth I, on the other hand, reportedly took a bath once a month (some quote it as twice a year) "whether she needed it or not."

This basic medical "fact"—that bathing would allow your body to let in diseases and thus kill you—persisted in Renaissance and Early Modern thinking for about three hundred years, which is why even people who could perfectly well afford hot baths often avoided them like the plague—for fear of catching the plague. According to contemporaries, King Henri IV of France (died 1610, from an assassin's knife, not disease) smelled like a goat—though he had so many mistresses that at least some women must have found his b.o. sexy.

Luckily, common sense prevailed eventually and frequent bathing—or at least washing—began to come back into fashion among the European middle and upper classes in the middle of the 18th century. Elaborate, luxurious bathrooms (meaning, of course, bathing rooms—privies were separate and often still are in older French buildings) became quite trendy in grand Parisian mansions and luxury apartment houses in the 1770s and 1780s. Still, Marie-Antoinette's courtiers, some of the older generation of whom probably smelled like barnyards, were bemused by her extravagant habit of taking a bath three times a week. And late-18th-century French feminist writer Olympe de Gouges was considered something between a madwoman and a whore because she bathed daily.

But even if you didn't stick to the Renaissance theory of disease via miasma, which made perfect sense at the time, there was an insurmountable practical obstacle that would have made even devoted bathers a bit odorous when fully dressed: the elaborate, heavy formal clothing of the Renaissance upper classes, made of costly and exotic cloth in rich, deep, expensive dyes—silk, velvet, brocade, cloth of gold. Today we'd dry-clean our silks and velvets, but in the Renaissance practically none of these clothes, except for the underclothing or "body linen," could be washed without ruining the fabrics or fading the dyes. (The fine outer clothing of earlier medieval times, and the everyday outer clothing of ordinary people, was more often made of woolen cloth, which can be hand washed without damaging it.)

The Tudor upper classes changed their body linen two or three times a day, in order to keep their outer clothing as fresh as possible, but eventually even outer clothing does pick up body odors. So, while fancy Renaissance and 17th- or 18th-century court clothing looked fabulous, after a dozen wearings it probably began to seem a little ripe, and after a year or so it must have smelled like a pig pen or the guy you were unfortunately sitting next to on the subway—and there was nothing anyone could do about keeping it clean except air it out, brush off dried dirt and stains as well as they could, and try to overcome the smell of unwashed clothing with lots of perfumes and herbal sachets.

Don't try so hard to be realistic that you make all your characters dirtier than they actually would have been. The idea that bathing was dangerous persisted in Europe—though not among everybody—from roughly the 1500s into the mid-to-late 1700s; at other times, your well-off characters would probably strive to be as clean as they could afford to be.

Table manners

A related myth about medieval and Renaissance Europe is the old cliché of everybody having barbaric table manners—eating with their hands any way they liked, and going after the food like pigs at a trough while dribbling gravy down their fronts. This one was undoubtedly aided and abetted by bad black-and-white movies—the image that comes to mind immediately is Charles Laughton in *The Private Life of Henry VIII*—where it's hilariously funny to us when all the knights, ladies, and even royalty sitting around the table in the great hall are chomping messily away at drumsticks held in their fists, and tossing bones over their shoulders for the dogs ("My, what boors those medieval people were!").

Nonsense.

The medieval and Renaissance upper classes had strict rules of etiquette. Granted, they weren't quite the same as ours, but gentlefolk were expected to abide by them. Table manners were important: Forks weren't generally used until the 18th century, but you were expected to cut up your portion of meat into small, refined pieces and there was a right and wrong way to eat it with your fingers, which were known as "God's Forks"—usually the proper way to take a morsel of food was with the second and third fingers and the thumb, leaving the first finger to discreetly cover the mouth while feeding oneself. Universal rules, which we'd find quite familiar, in etiquette books from the 15th and 16th centuries included *No belching, spitting, or picking your teeth (with either fingers or knife) at the table; No elbows on the table; No over-filling your mouth; No dipping pieces of meat in the shared salt dish; No drinking without first wiping the traces of gravy or grease from your mouth.*

An illustration from a 15th-century printing of *The Canterbury Tales.*

The people who did have poor table manners and boorish personal habits tended to be, as you might expect, the peasant, laboring, and lower-middle classes. And, not coincidentally, those etiquette books started appearing in libraries in the late fifteenth century, when capitalism was hitting its stride and the newly rich merchants and bankers—who might have started life in very humble circumstances—needed to learn how to sit down with the nobility and not make fools of themselves, with such firm suggestions as "Do not spit upon the floor or blow your nose into your hand in company"—and lots more.

Tall people and small people

Another myth that's become popular among people who have done some casual studying of the past, particularly of historical clothing that's survived into our century, is that people in past eras were all stunted, undernourished little runts. That one's about half true.

However, the farther back you go, the less likely it is that genuine items of clothing will survive. The greater part of our costume archives is made up of clothing from the 18th century and later. And the trouble with that is that we look at an incredibly petite Victorian woman's dress in a museum and assume that everybody in every century was the same tiny size as that long-dead woman.

First, though, we have to keep in mind that the clothing that lasted long enough to end up in a museum today was usually the clothing of the middle and upper classes. For most of human history, the clothing of peasants, hard manual laborers, and really poor people was generally handed down to a family member or sold to the old-clothes man and was re-sold and re-used and mended and altered for years until it finally reached the point of uselessness and fell completely apart and was sold to the ragman for recycling at the paper mill. So we have far fewer examples of the clothing of the poor, especially before the Industrial Revolution, and of their dress sizes.

Lots of 18th/19th-century people were tiny, because lots of the 18th/19th-century people whose clothing might have survived—the upper class, the professional and mercantile middle class, and the lower middle class of small tradesmen, skilled artisans, and so on, lived in cities. Urban people have been traditionally looked upon by country folk as scrawny and effete. One reason for that is the limited diet of the urban lower classes of almost any era, and another is that many urban jobs in an early industrial society (and in the luxury trades that usually were located in cities, near the customers—the rich) required skill, rather than the brute strength and endurance that farming did. A skinny, 5'3" male wood carver or 4'10" female embroiderer can get just as much done in a day as a 6'2" wood carver or 5'8" embroiderer can—and needs to eat less to survive. Members of the upper class, on the other hand, who got plenty to eat, didn't need to be physically husky by the late Renaissance—few of them were out actually swinging battleaxes when they were at war—and so genetically smaller and slighter aristocrats got to pass their genes along to the next generation.

Poor or moderately poor urban people, who made up at least 80% of most urban populations from ancient Rome onward, tended to have fairly monotonous diets because their food had to be transported into the cities and what the poor could afford wasn't that fresh (they also had to stick to food items that were less perishable and therefore cheaper, which is why cabbage became known as the food of the poor, while the rich were eating spinach and watercress). They didn't get many vitamins or healthy foods at the best of times—the poor Victorians, for instance, got most of their protein from fried fish and chips. Urban workers, servants, and the like in the 18th and 19th centuries did tend to be small, a combination of genes and limited diet; the height of the average 18th-century male Parisian worker was about 5'3".

Their country cousins, however, were still doing hard manual work and were closer to the food they were eating, and they were bigger and sturdier, as were their neighbors who were building houses or heaving coal at the docks—they had to be.

Cro-Magnon bones found by paleontologists show us that our Stone Age European ancestors of thirty or fifty thousand years ago were, on average, actually an inch or two taller and more muscular than 21st-century Europeans and North Americans, for all our scientific nutritional analyses and vitamin supplements. Part of this is undoubtedly due to the fact that the Stone Age hunter-gatherers were very, very close to their food—pick a leaf and eat it, kill a mammoth and eat it—and so got the maximum value of its freshness, not to mention that the food was entirely natural, organic, and un-messed-around-with; their animal protein was extra-lean wild game with very little fat except at certain times of the year. The other factor here is Darwinian selection—unless a Cro-Magnon male was a big husky fellow, he wasn't going to be much of a spear hunter. And while the clan or tribe probably wouldn't have let the skinny guy starve because he was better suited for basket weaving or snaring rabbits than hunting mammoth, bison, and cave bears, a slightly built Cro-Magnon male would have been a less desirable mate, and most likely got fewer chances to pass along his genes to the next generation.

Fine. What about people in recorded history rather than prehistory?

Your average ancient, medieval, and preindustrial peasant was physically working just as hard as those Cro-Magnon hunters—perhaps harder—to feed himself, pay his dues to whomever ran his local castle or province, and keep a roof of some kind over his head. He had the help of domesticated animals and clever inventions like canal irrigation, windmills, and water wheels, but essentially he was doing one heck of a lot of manual labor to keep himself and his family alive, and the natural selection that went for Cro-Magnons undoubtedly went for Roman farmers and 16th-century German peasants as well. A big muscular man (or woman) can work a field better than a puny one can, and can produce more food for his/her family, which means that everyone's a little better nourished and taller and stronger, and so it goes. And while the peasants were out of luck if the harvest was bad or armies in the latest civil war trampled their crops, and were probably chronically undernourished in comparison to the nobility, they simply couldn't have done the work they did every day without being pretty good physical specimens.

Their medieval lords, meanwhile, were much better fed and were all expected to take a hand in fighting for their king and to ride a war horse and swing a broadsword or a spiked mace in the midst of the troops. Medieval kings, aristocrats, and knights were the least likely people of all to be undersized. William the Conqueror, for example, was about 5'10" tall, scarcely a runt (though his queen, Matilda, was petite, about 5' tall—not 4'2" as has been erroneously reported). Edward I of England (1239-1307), who was called "Longshanks" on account of his height and long legs, stood 6'2". Charlemagne was 6'3".[23] Jumping forward a few centuries, George Washington also stood about 6'3". While these examples may have been out of the ordinary for their time, such measurements certainly weren't unheard-of.

As the centuries passed, however, and being a magnificent fighter with a broadsword or battleaxe was no longer an absolute requirement for a member of the aristocracy, petite members of the nobility also got to pass their genes along. By the Renaissance, a slender, refined build was considered just as attractive as a husky, sword-swinging build—and it distinguished you nicely from the husky, scythe-swinging peasants. (There's a reason that, by the 18th century, aristocrats fought duels with pistols or rapiers—it's unlikely that many of them could have hefted a medieval broadsword.)

Aside: What about Napoleon? Wasn't *he* a little shrimp—practically a midget?

Aaaarghhhh!

The short answer: NO. Do stop swallowing movie clichés, if you please!

Napoleon was not a tiny little posturing runt. While he wasn't in George Washington's outsize height class, he was about 5'6" or 5'7", which, if you look back a few paragraphs, was about three or four inches taller than the average working-class Parisian of the 18th century and was a respectable height for his time and place (the French and Italians are still, apparently genetically, on average a smaller, leaner people than their Germanic neighbors).

These myths about Napoleon being a runt in his own time

---

[23] All these measurements were taken during actual exhumations and medical examinations of their skeletons during the past two hundred years.

are pop culture clichés, originating from propaganda (*Don't Just Swallow the Propaganda, Clichés, and Myths*) spread by his many enemies across Europe, particularly the British conservative press. These are the same enemies who tried to spread the rumor that he was practically a peasant and that he had begun his military career as a common corporal, when, in fact, he was a member of a minor noble family, had attended the elite École Militaire (royal military academy) in Paris, and began his career as a commissioned officer in an artillery regiment.

Teeth

Yet another lingering myth about premodern people (probably also taken from movies) is that they all, especially the ragged poor of the ancient world and the Middle Ages, had terrible, rotten teeth—presumably from a lack of toothpaste and modern dentistry. Nothing could be farther from the truth. What's closer to the truth is that many of the *upper classes* had terrible teeth. Look at a portrait of Napoleon's empress Joséphine sometime. It's said that her habitual, enigmatic little closed-mouth smile that people found so alluring was actually a result of her having ugly, decaying or downright rotten, teeth (though the tooth decay may have been a result of bad hygiene and bad nutrition while she was imprisoned during the Terror, but growing up on sugar plantations in the West Indies couldn't have helped much); she didn't dare smile a big, toothy grin in public.

Look back in Chapter 9, "Money," and reread the history of sugar in Europe. The great majority of Europeans had no concentrated source of sugar, except honey, in their diet for thousands of years—sugar was imported from Asia and was insanely expensive. And you don't get a huge amount of honey from keeping bees at the best of times, so honey was a fairly valuable commodity.

We've all heard from our mothers and our dentists how too much sugar will rot our teeth. Poor people before the late

17th century may have had inadequate nutrition that didn't do their teeth any good, and may have had teeth knocked out or broken in the course of their harsh lives, and had only rags or twigs with which to clean their teeth at the best of times; but their diets were almost entirely lacking that big, bad hobgoblin, refined sugar—plus its cheap and ubiquitous modern cousin, corn syrup, helped along by soft, pasty white breads that all have (yes) sugar added—that will do much worse damage to adult teeth than nutritional deficiencies ever will.

Because ordinary ancient folk and Europeans, until the late 17th century or so, had such limited access to sugar, tooth decay, meaning cavities, wasn't much of a problem for them—while ancient Roman, and European medieval, aristocrats bought and enjoyed their expensive, imported sugar and also had a much higher rate of toothache. (Though at least the wealthier of the ancient Etruscans, after having aching teeth pulled, could afford some primitive dentistry: archaeologists have actually discovered some examples of ancient dentures and bridgework, made of gold wire and fake teeth hand-carved from cattle bone.) So the wealthy were the ones who were really suffering from bad teeth, until the middle and working classes began to join them in the Rotten Teeth Club during the two centuries, roughly late 1600s to late 1800s, that featured a ruinous combination of (a) easier/cheaper access to sugar and (b) no dental care for the poor beyond extraction.

How do we know all this? From archaeology. Skeletal remains of Stone Age Europeans show worn teeth, broken teeth, poorly developed teeth—but hardly any decayed teeth. The same goes for the teeth of ordinary Egyptian mummies and of the many poor and middle-class people whose skeletons were found at Pompeii and Herculaneum. Even the teeth of the skeletons of the dozens of sailors who went down with the *Mary Rose*, Henry VIII's flagship that sank in 1545 and was raised in 1982, were found to be in remarkably good condition. (A scholarly paper about ancient Etruscan and Roman medicine mentions that only 4% of the ancient Mediterranean teeth a particular anthropologist studied showed decay[24]—

while it's a good guess, on the other hand, that fewer than 4% of modern, sugar-saturated adult Westerners *don't* have any tooth decay.) Though it's unlikely that many of the poor of the ancient world, the Middle Ages, or the Renaissance had perfect teeth by the time they reached thirty, it is likely that they were still in better shape than those of the sugar-eating rich.

---

[24] Weiss, Morris, M.D., "Etruscan Origins" [of ancient Roman medicine], published online by the Innominate Society of Louisville. The article also describes the Etruscan dentures. http://innominatesociety.com/online/

14

More Anachronisms of Attitude: Servants—Not a Luxury, a Necessity

once had the wonderful experience of being "historical advisor" to an excellent community theater production of Molière's comedy *The Miser* (first performed in 1668). The play, as you can guess, is about a miser, his lovelorn son and daughter, his grumpy, underpaid servants, and his beloved money box, and it's full of very funny wisecracks and sight gags about just how stingy Monsieur Harpagon is. So one of the questions that a cast member asked me during rehearsals was: "If Harpagon is so stingy, why does he employ at least four servants? Would he spend so much money on a luxury like that?"

I answered, "No matter how stingy you are, you'd have a vacuum cleaner in your house, wouldn't you, even if it was a cheap, old, beat-up, not very good one? It's just something you need and wouldn't even think about, isn't it?"

The problem with 21st-century attitudes about servants is that we imagine them all to be the hordes of crisp, uniformed types we see in *Downton Abbey* (or *Upstairs, Downstairs* if you're a generation older) or read about in every other 1930s stately-home mystery; and their employers to be fabulously rich folks who always had their breakfast in bed (served, of course, by the lady's maid or ruffle-aproned parlormaid). People with servants today are socialites, in Park Avenue apartments or Beverly Hills mansions, who speak condescendingly about "the help." "Servant" has become a rather politically incorrect word and it conjures up vast wealth, curtsying housemaids, butlers wearing tailcoats and carrying silver trays, and everything else we can recall from *Masterpiece Theatre*—while nobody *we* know has ever been rich enough to afford a live-in servant.

Right?

Actually, even if you don't have a cleaning lady in from time to time to get the dust out of the corners, or a yard service stopping by to mow your lawn and clip your hedges, you probably have at least seven servants in your house at this minute. Three live in your basement, three in your kitchen, and one in your broom closet. Of course, they're made of metal and motors and wiring, not flesh and blood, and they're called Furnace, Water Heater, Washing Machine, Dishwasher,

Food Processor (or Blender or Mixer), Gas/Electric Range, and Vacuum Cleaner instead of Sarah, Peggy, or Gladys, but they're still servants.

With our mechanical servants and added conveniences such as preserved and prepared foods, we in the 21st century tend to forget what a lot of basic human-muscle work it takes to feed a family and maintain a clean, respectable, comfortable middle-class home, let alone a grand and gracious aristocratic one. But if you don't have an automatic, oil- or gas-fed, furnace and water heater, you need a servant to help you set fires and clean out fireplaces and keep the kitchen fire going to heat water for bathing, cooking, and washing the dishes and the clothes. If you don't have a refrigerator, you need a cook or kitchenmaid to go to the market every day to buy fresh provisions for the day's meals, which have to be cooked fresh every day, for leftovers won't keep long (they weren't wasted—the servants got those). If you don't have a vacuum cleaner, it takes two or three people with brooms far longer to sweep all the floors and beat the carpets than it would have taken one person to clean them with an Electrolux. Et cetera.

So imagine now that you are an upper-middle-income housewife in a biggish house (have to keep up with the neighbors) with a husband, five or six children ranging in age from one to fourteen, probably at least one elderly parent living with you, and one impoverished, middle-aged, "old maid" female relative who "needs a home" and has taken over the smaller spare bedroom. Do you think you could possibly manage to keep the house clean and warm, the clothes tidy, and feed everyone every day with meals made entirely from scratch without the help of all those mechanical servants?

Wealthy families employed the butler, the footmen, and the ruffle-aproned parlormaids for show (conspicuous consumption is nothing new), but most servants, throughout the centuries, were simply all the extra hands who were needed to keep anything but the poorest, simplest household running smoothly. Until World War II, nearly every family of any size with a middle-class income or more, even the household of, for instance, a single, well-off professional such as a bachelor lawyer, had at least a couple of servants to do the cooking and cleaning, usually a live-in cook and housemaid. A small household with a more modest income would often have "daily help" who came in most days of the week for a few morning hours.

A well-off, but not by any means fabulously wealthy, household would have several more servants, at least half a dozen. The Bantrys in Agatha Christie's *The Body in the Library*, written around 1941 but set sometime before the beginning of World War II, are a middle-aged, apparently childless couple, typical members of the post-Victorian landowning gentry, living in comfortable circumstances with a sizeable country house and working estate—though nothing like the enormous and lavish scale of, say, *Downton Abbey*. The two of them are the only residents of the house and they probably don't entertain much or host large weekend houseparties, but they have at least five servants to keep everything running properly—a butler, a cook, and three housemaids are mentioned in the novel, and probably there are also a kitchenmaid and a boot boy (an adolescent who did messy jobs like cleaning shoes) lurking somewhere "below stairs."[25]

Servants weren't a luxury. Like a vacuum cleaner today, throughout most of human history they were a simple necessity for the household of lower-middle-class status or above, and most—depending on their level of training, competence, and classiness—were cheap, working for little more than their board and lodging. (One of the "stinginess jokes" in *The Miser* is that Harpagon expects his [male] cook—a busy, full-time job—to act also as his coachman . . . for no additional pay, of course.)

---

[25] Agatha Christie's many novels are a terrific resource for details on upper-middle-class-blending-into-minor-aristocracy British life and households in the first half of the 20th century; Christie had lived all her early life in that world and was "writing what she knew."

The urban people in past centuries who were too poor to employ a servant, on the other hand, had children to do the chores (they weren't wasting their time in school) and usually were also too poor to live in more than one room for a family of eight or ten—one room doesn't take long to sweep. They didn't have a kitchen for a servant to work in, or much of any kind of cooking area beyond a simple hearth—if they had a fireplace at all; that would have involved paying a higher rent on their overcrowded lodgings. Such people lived mostly on bread, soup (or other one-pot stews), and cheap, portable street food. (And it was from this poorest, subsistence-level class that most ordinary domestic servants came.)

Christie's *The Murder at the Vicarage* (1930) features a highly entertaining but doubtless very true-to-life portrayal of the sort of servant that middle-class people at the lower end of the income scale would have had, right into the 20th century. Sloppy, uncouth, barely trained and mostly incompetent maid of all work/cook Mary is employed by the vicar and his wife, Griselda, who have a servant as a matter of course because they couldn't manage without one, but who are too poor to afford anyone better. Mary, who probably only wears a shabby uniform when her employers have company to dinner, and otherwise moodily knocks about in a grubby apron, is a far cry from the correct, spotless, deferential housemaids of *Downton Abbey*:

> "Is that all?" said Mary. "Because what I mean to say is I've got the joint in the oven and the pudding boiling over as likely as not."
>
> … She left the room, and I turned to Griselda.
>
> "Is it quite out of the question to induce Mary to say sir or ma'am?"
>
> "I have told her. She doesn't remember. She's just a raw girl, remember?"
>
> "I am perfectly aware of that," I said. "But raw things do not necessarily remain raw for ever. I feel a tinge of cooking might be induced in Mary."
>
> "Well, I don't agree with you," said Griselda. "You know how little we can afford to pay a servant. If once we got her smartened up at all, she'd leave. Naturally. And get higher wages. But as long as Mary can't cook and has those awful manners—well, we're safe, nobody else would have her."
>
> … Whether it was worth while having a maid at the price of her not being able to cook, and having a habit of throwing dishes and remarks at one with the same disconcerting abruptness, was a debatable matter. … I confess that I have a hankering after a room thoroughly dusted and tidied every morning. Mary's practice of flicking off the more obvious deposit on the surface of low tables is to my thinking grossly inadequate.

Only the wealthy, however, expected the servants to do *all* the work. The lower-middle-class housewife's "girl" (generally a maid of all work, who also did the cooking), for example, wasn't doing the purchasing, food prep, cooking, and washing up while the mistress of the house sat about and ate bonbons or gossiped over tea or visited her dressmaker. She was *assisting* the mistress of the house and her daughters in getting through all the necessary, everyday work—including, but not limited to, cleaning house with only a feather duster, some rags, a mop, and a broom; making beds and airing or restuffing mattresses; lugging firewood or coal and setting fires in every room that required one for warmth (and cleaning the grate, a hard, filthy job with coal fires); and especially cooking, serving meals, and cleaning up afterward, which entailed a lot of messy, tedious work—peeling, trimming, chopping, boning; lugging, heating, and dumping water; washing pots and dishes; building and maintaining the kitchen fire—that all our dozens of different electrical kitchen appliances and gadgets, plus our running water and drain pipes, do for us now. And then there was always the laundry.

Don't fool yourself: today, the kitchenmaids are still around, chopping the vegetables and washing the dishes. They've merely turned into the food processor and the dishwasher, which do much the same work for us but don't ask for a salary, need to be fed daily, or get "in trouble" after flirting with the footman.

Until the early 19th century, a job as a servant, even if only of the "general household drudge" variety in a lower-middle-class household, was something that semi-literate teen-aged girls from the countryside or the back streets took as a matter of course. In 19th-century America, poor immigrants—the lowest rung of the social ladder, especially with the vast influx of Irish peasants fleeing the potato famine in the 1840s—often filled the positions. And the men and women (mostly women) with jobs as servants in ordinary households were glad to get the jobs, since a live-in position in service, despite the low pay and hard, unending physical work, still generally offered better food and lodging than they would find at home in the squalid, desperately poor urban slums or rural villages from which most of them came.

It was only when industrialization was hitting its stride that unmarried working-class girls had a real alternative, a job in the local mill, to being in service; but factory jobs, though they had shorter hours, often paid less (when you factored in the room and board supplied with a live-in domestic job) and could be much more dangerous. In Victorian England, and into the 1920s and 30s, working-class mothers often encouraged their teenaged daughters to go into domestic service for a few years, not necessarily with any intention of remaining in service for the rest of their lives: It was safer than mill-work, plus working as a maid of all work, kitchenmaid, or housemaid was essentially a home economics course—good training and practice for the inevitable housekeeping and cooking the girl would be doing when she eventually married.

Aside: What's the difference between a housemaid and a parlormaid?

In large, wealthy Victorian households, there were strict divisions of servants' roles and duties. A housemaid was a cleaning lady; she swept, dusted, polished furniture, changed and made beds, beat rugs, tidied up, and generally kept the house presentable. If there wasn't a younger, subordinate maid who'd get stuck with the worst, dirtiest jobs, a housemaid would also clean the fireplace grates and lay and light fires in the mornings. Housemaids did not, as a rule, interact much with their employers; they were expected to keep out of sight while performing their duties.

A parlormaid, on the other hand, was a glorified waitress with refined manners, usually young and attractive, who was employed to impress people; she'd serve sandwiches at afternoon tea, offer the vegetables at dinner (though not at really grand households, where etiquette decreed that only male servants—footmen—were supposed to wait at table), and answer the front door if the butler was occupied. Households too modest to employ a full-time parlormaid often had house-parlormaids, who worked as housemaids in the morning and then, in the afternoon, with a change of uniform to something a bit less drab, doubled as parlormaids when visitors came to tea.

15

Bloopers: Guillotines—and the Obligatory Heart-Wrenching French Revolution Execution Scene

ou just knew I had to get to this one eventually, didn't you?

(If you're squeamish, feel free to skip ahead to Chapter 16.)

The closest most of us will ever get to a guillotine is, fortunately, in the movies. *Un*fortunately, most movies, even French movies, manage to get them at least slightly wrong. And while most authors can figure out the basics of how a guillotine works—its blade drops down and chops off your head, right?—they usually make a mess of it when they try to go into details of either the machine or the ritual of the 18th-century French public execution.

On the following page is a pair of sketches. Figure A is a very good, accurate, and properly proportioned rendition of a real, working French guillotine, probably a late-19th-century model.[26] Figure B, on the other hand, is a tragic joke.

The minor detail that 99% of movies manage to get wrong (*Do Not Borrow Your Period Details & Information From*

---

[26] Though most people think of it as purely a French Revolution prop, the guillotine was the sole official method of execution used in France and French territories until the death penalty was abolished; its last use was in 1977.

Other People's Historical Novels & Movies…) is the rope. In Figure B, you can see that the rope is attached to the top of the blade, is run through an eye bolt or something, and falls back down to the ground, presumably for the convenience of the guy who has to heave the blade up again after a chop. (No easy task: the blade, with its attached weight which is the dark thing above the triangular blade in Figure A and which is, unsurprisingly, missing in Figure B, weighs at least 90 pounds.)

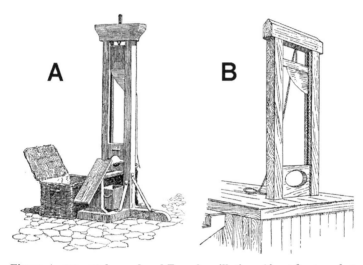

Figure A, accurately rendered French guillotine: About fourteen feet high and 2.5 feet wide; heavy drop-weight (*mouton*) bolted to top of blade; tilting plank (*bascule*) and proper attached platform for sliding the *bascule* along to place victim beneath blade; release lever at the side of the uprights. **Figure B, cartoon guillotine:** About seven feet high. Too broad and squat. No *mouton*. No *bascule*. *Lunette* placed so victim must lie flat on the platform. Blade released by a simple rope which remains attached. Pathetic.

A real guillotine blade, when it's ready to drop, **has no rope attached to it**, in order to be sure that nothing whatsoever will impede its fall. The blade is never attached to *anything* when it falls. It's held in place above by a double hook, rather like a "lobster claw" jewelry clasp, which pops open when the executioner tugs the lever which releases a spring catch. He never "releases the rope," as some novels breathlessly tell us, to let the blade fall, because There. Is. No. Rope. To. Release. (A rope is, naturally, used to haul the blade up again. *The rope is then completely detached from the blade* once the blade is in place and secured by the double hook.)

Remarkably, Hollywood got it right at least twice: MGM's 1935 *A Tale of Two Cities* and their 1938 *Marie Antoinette*, which clearly shared the same prop guillotine, have a mostly accurate machine, complete with lobster-claw catch that releases a ropeless, weighted blade. No doubt for dramatic effect, however, the blade is too massive (it looks about an inch thick; a genuine blade is roughly ⅓" thick) and the whole machine is far too tall, apparently about twenty feet high, while a real 1790s guillotine stood about twelve to fourteen feet high.

Regrettably, the best and most comprehensive French Revolution movie ever made, the two-part *La Révolution Française* (1989), does have a rope attached to its guillotine blade!

You wouldn't think that anyone could get the function of the tilting plank (the *bascule*)—on which the victim lies face down and is then slid under the blade—hilariously wrong, but one author of a terribly earnest historical novel did, in spades. This author, no doubt influenced by what he knew of Tudor beheadings, evidently had never seen even a bad French Revolution movie and had not the faintest idea that you lie flat on your stomach to be guillotined. Nevertheless, he felt he had to describe an execution in minute detail, and so carefully depicted his victim kneeling, butt in the air, in front of the guillotine as one might have knelt at a Tudor block. And then, since he had obviously consulted a picture of a real guillotine but couldn't quite figure out the purpose of that board thing, had them tilt the *bascule* down *over* the victim and secure it so that the victim's rump and his back were "locked in position."

Good grief.

Naturally, the *bascule* is totally absent in our Figure B. Sure, it's a piece of cake to get a (possibly struggling) victim to lie down on the platform and obligingly stick his neck under the blade, right? Not to mention that the engineering-challenged artist forgot to leave a space for the blade to land after it's sliced through a neck at extremely high speed. Maybe it's just supposed to leave dents in the floor.

The artist who drew Figure B, and far too many authors who have mentioned victims "kneeling" in front of a guillotine, were probably misled by pictures of the original medieval or Early Modern beheading machines on which the modern guillotine was based, the English "Halifax gibbet," the Scottish "Maiden," or the *mannaia* of the Italian Renaissance. None of these had a *bascule* and victims did presumably kneel beneath them. There's also a rather sentimental and prettified engraving that circulated in 1789-90, when Dr. Joseph-Ignace Guillotin first put forward the idea of a humane beheading

 device to the French National Assembly, which was overhauling the penal code to abolish cruel execution methods. The proposed machine in the 1789 picture is a French artist's barely-updated version of the "Halifax gibbet" or the "Maiden," last used in the 17th century: The machine in the print isn't nearly tall enough to provide an effective chop, the executioner (eyes decently averted) is going to cut a rope with a sword to release the blade, there's no *bascule*, and the victim is, yes, kneeling at the machine.

That's *1789*, folks: this well-known picture was created *three years before* the official French guillotine was designed

and built in 1792, without the artist ever laying his eyes on anything of the sort. Do not refer to it for information for your 1793 execution scene!

But when the genuine, working French guillotine was created,[27] it was designed with speed, efficiency, humanity, and, not least, convenience for the executioners in mind. And "convenient" for an 18th-century French executioner, when the point of an execution with the new-fangled guillotine was now to dispatch the victim swiftly and painlessly rather than to drag the process out in torture as they'd been doing it for centuries, was to be able to get the whole thing done with as little fuss and effort as possible. So, aside from the angled blade, which cuts better than a horizontal blade does (ask an engineer about it), the *bascule* was the most significant and useful improvement to the original medieval model. It's much easier and faster to push someone—or two or three some-ones in succession—against a plank standing, and then strap them on, tilt them over, and slide them forward, than it is to wrestle them to the ground one by one and force them to kneel or lie long enough in one place to let the blade do its work.

One of the worst "historical" novels set in the French Revolution that I ever tried to read began with the mass guillotining of an aristocratic family. Yes, this happened a few times during the *Grande Terreur* (June-July 1794). But what *never, ever* happened was a mass guillotining at the *beginning* of the Revolution, and . . . inside the family's own home.

Say what???

This author, whom I mentioned briefly in *Don't Just Swallow the Propaganda, Clichés, & Myths*, doesn't have a single clue about the French Revolution, much less about guillotines, and clearly doesn't care. Besides all the other big honk-

---

[27] By one Tobias Schmidt, an inventor, tinkerer, and piano maker, based on drawings of the Scottish and Italian machines but with several improvements suggested by Charles Sanson, the master executioner, and Dr. Antoine Louis, the king's physician.

ing historical inaccuracies that she manages to pack into her first two pages, her execution scene, intended to shock and affect us with the butchering of innocent young girls in extremely purple prose, is so totally over-the-top wrong that it's just plain funny.

Her cartoon guillotine straight out of Figure B, which is being used dozens of times a day in 1789 (when no aristocratic families whatsoever were being butchered wholesale by any method and—oh, right—*when the French guillotine would not be conceived, decreed, or built for another three years*) is rolled on wheels, completely assembled, along the streets and pushed inside our poor, blameless aristos' grand mansions. At which point, in the worst home invasion ever, the poor, blameless aristos get promptly bundled to the machine by the indispensable evil, grinning, smelly sansculottes[28] (without a trial, of course—the author never heard of the Revolutionary Tribunal, either) and lose their heads inside their own elegant salons. And bloodstains are so hard to get out of the carpet.

In how many other ways is this whole absurd scene a few miles wide of the mark?

Executions, before, during, and after the French Revolution and until the last French public execution in 1939 (yes, that's not a typo, *nineteen-thirty-nine*), *always* took place in a spot specifically determined by the city government. On a raised scaffold in full public view (they lowered the platform to ground level in the mid 19th century). Because part of the ritual of 18th-century and revolutionary justice (and 19th-century justice, and 17th-century justice, and 16th-century justice . . .) was the highly visible and public carrying out of that justice, to impress onlookers with the power of the law, and to deter potential criminals. Aside from all this, a guillotine was an expensive piece of equipment, paid for by the state and kept under lock and key by the official executioner;

---

[28] Working-class Parisians of the revolutionary era. The name comes from their everyday costume: laborers and artisans usually wore sturdy trousers of the modern sort on work days, while aristocrats, the rich, and the middle class wore knee breeches (*culottes*; *sans culotte* = "without breeches").

bloodthirsty mobs, if they suddenly felt like committing a little violence, couldn't possibly just get their hands on one and schlep it around Paris for vindictive choppings—even if one had existed when this author blithely declares it did.

All those poor aristocrats must have had mighty tall doors to allow that fantasy rolling guillotine (fourteen feet high, remember, plus the fantasy wheels, of course) into the parlor. Needless to say—please, *please* take my word for this—there is no such thing, and never was any such thing, as a rolling guillotine anywhere outside a magician's stage set or a particularly schlocky horror movie. A precision piece of machinery like a guillotine, designed to do its job with the greatest speed, accuracy, and reliability possible, was never intended to be pushed (fully assembled) like a shopping cart along cobblestoned streets. (I'll also add that a real one is not hard to take apart, transport, and reassemble; it takes only about half an hour to put one together properly.[29])

So, if a character in your novel is about to be guillotined in Paris during the Terror, here's the whole process, the way it actually would have happened, from prison to the scaffold in the Place de la Révolution:

A. Condemned prisoners wait in the preparation room ("*salle de toilette*") of the Conciergerie prison (now a museum and historic landmark; do visit it if you're in Paris), for anywhere between one and twenty-four hours after being condemned to death at the Revolutionary Tribunal upstairs at the Law Courts. They do not get taken back to the cells in which they've spent the last day or two before trial. When the executioners arrive, the prisoners get their hair cut short above their necks; their cravats removed and usually also their coats

---

[29] As demonstrated in text and photos by a handful of volunteers in a chapter of *Paroles de Bourreau* (Paris, Editions Imago, 2002), a memoir by Fernand Meyssonnier (1931-2008), France's last living executioner. Visit his French Wikipedia page for a photo of him with a genuine 19th-century guillotine. http://fr.wikipedia.org/wiki/Fernand_Meyssonnier

and waistcoats, unless it's a cold day; their shirt collars cut away (or, for ladies, their fichus or kerchiefs removed); and their hands tied behind their backs.

The tied hands (for the sake of impeding the prisoners and preventing them from resisting or escaping—come on, you've all watched cop shows, for heaven's sake) and the haircut and the cut-away shirt (to be sure that nothing what-soever obstructed the blade, for a clean, painless chop) *are not negotiable.* No guillotine victim, during the French Revolu-tion or at any time during the two centuries afterward, ever went to the scaffold with her luxuriant three-foot-long hair floating romantically about her in the breeze, or (as Dickens touchingly but erroneously tells us in *A Tale of Two Cities*) holding hands with another prisoner, unless they were incon-veniently, uncomfortably, and rather ridiculously back-to-back.

Alas, in the highly disappointing 1980 TV-movie version of *Two Cities*, Sydney Carton goes under the blade with his coat on, his shoulder-length hair hanging loose, AND with about six thick layers of knotted linen cravat wound around his throat. To which the only possible response can be, "Are they *kidding*???"

Just to make it all even sillier, most film versions of *A Tale of Two Cities* or *The Scarlet Pimpernel* actually have their condemned aristocrats riding stoically in the (open-ended) tumbrils through Paris with their hands free, looking more like bored tourists on a sightseeing bus than people under sen-tence of imminent death. Wouldn't you think that at least one of them, completely unencumbered like that, would just jump out and make a dash for it?[30]

B. Condemned prisoners ride (standing, or sitting on a plank bench provided, if they prefer) in a tumbril through the streets of Paris to the Place de la Révolution, now Place de la Concorde. This journey was not devised during the Terror for

---

[30] Again, the 1935 *A Tale of Two Cities* does manage to get it right, with everyone tied up properly, although there are a lot of condemned prisoners still wearing cravats and pigtailed powdered wigs in the background . . .

the purpose of humiliating condemned aristocrats (or of providing future historical novelists with an opportunity to write a good, juicy, long-drawn-out farewell scene loaded with pathos). Criminals going to execution had invariably been carted in elaborate processions through the streets from prison to public scaffold, in a calculated display of authority at work, for hundreds of years before the Revolution—just as criminals about to be hanged in 18th-century London had a long ride from Newgate Prison to the gallows at Tyburn ahead of them. ("Tumbril," by the way, is just an old-fashioned word for "farm cart"—French *tombereau*—specifically a two-wheeled open cart, and neither the thing nor the word was invented as some sinister symbol of the Terror. English farmers hauling manure or cabbages in 1750 had tumbrils, too.)

Parisians shout rude comments as the carts pass and sometimes a spirited victim shouts something rude or clever back. Parisians do *not* throw nasty things such as dead rats or rotten vegetables at the prisoners because the carts are always surrounded by a military escort of mounted *gendarmerie*, who are there to keep order and who have a strong objection to having things thrown at them.

Regarding the "howling mobs" of Parisians, the near-daily execution processions during the Terror soon became "old hat" for locals—executions before the Revolution had averaged one per month or so—and those huge crowds of movie extras rarely appeared unless someone quite famous or unpopular was about to be "shortened." The average execution of a handful of individuals (before the *Grande Terreur* of June-July 1794) was rarely attended by more than a hundred or so curious onlookers—not the cheering, bloodthirsty thousands who fill the square in movies. [31]

C. If there's more than one prisoner to be executed, as-

---

[31] Look closely at the 1793 painting *Une Exécution Capitale, Place de la Révolution* [www.carnavalet.paris.fr/en/collections/une-execution-capitale-place-de-la-revolution ; click "Agrandir" beneath the painting to enlarge], and you'll see that the onlookers are standing only about three or four deep around the scaffold.

sistant executioners (***not*** "guards," soldiers, or any member of any uniformed escort; owing to the social stigma under which executioners labored, no one in uniform would have *ever* directly participated in an execution) arrange the prisoners into a line, backs to the guillotine so they can't see it in action. The order in which they are to be executed is determined by the prosecutor right after the trial, usually with women first and with any famous prisoners reserved for last.

With very, very few exceptions, the executioners treated the prisoners with respect and did not taunt them, handle them roughly, or drag out the process to prolong the misery. They had an ugly job to do, but it was part of their "professional ethics" to do the job quickly and humanely.

D. The victim climbs up to the scaffold and is firmly but gently shoved by the executioners against the *bascule*, which is in its standing position, leaning at a slight angle against its framework, toward the guillotine's upright beams.

E. Still standing and leaning forward against the *bascule*, the victim is secured onto it with a couple of straps at elbow- and knee-level so he can't wriggle out of place at the wrong moment.

F. The *bascule* is tipped forward and down, like a see-saw, to horizontal. It is then slid forward along its supporting framework (sometimes little wheels beneath it make this easier) until his neck is positioned above the lower half of the *lunette*, the little round cutout.

G. The top half of the *lunette* is dropped into place above the neck, immobilizing it.

H. The chief executioner pulls the lever which releases the 90-pound blade. *Thunk.* A *lot* of blood spurts out; severing a few major arteries and veins all at once is a messy business. (The only recent movie that ever came close to showing the true bloodiness of the process is Andrzej Wajda's 1982 *Danton*, whose execution scene is pretty graphic.)

Your character's head falls into a leather sack, not a basket—though the decapitated body plus head would then be immediately placed in a coffin-like wicker basket for transportation to the burial ground—see Figure A. Only during the final two or three months of the Terror, during the daily mass executions of twenty or more, were the bodies and heads flung higgledy-piggledy into a waiting, straw-lined cart; it would have been impractical and impossible to provide enough body baskets.

The nonfiction author who luridly described the potential horror, during a mass execution, of looking down from your place on the guillotine into "a basket full of severed heads" had far too vivid an imagination; both trunk and head were swiftly removed from sight. Part of the executioners' considerate treatment of the prisoners was, during a multiple execution, to remove as many traces as possible of the previous execution, including a quick wipe-down of the equipment before the next victim arrived on the platform. Shocking and horrifying a "patient" at the last instant with the ghastly experience of looking down into a basketful of bloody heads would not have been entertained for a moment:

> When six heads had fallen, the baskets and the *bascule* were so covered with blood that the contact of this blood must have seemed more horrible than death itself to those who followed. My grandfather ordered two aides to throw buckets of water on the *bascule* and to sponge down the parts after each execution.
>
> [from *Sept Générations d'Exécuteurs* (1862), by Clément Sanson]

And finally, if you're thinking about climaxing your story with a dramatic last-minute rescue of your heroine from beneath the guillotine blade as it starts to fall, please do think again and rewrite the scene so that she's rescued from the cart on the way to the public scaffold. Why?

Your hero is going to have a very hard time stopping the guillotine blade in mid-drop. He can't grab the rope to stop the blade because, as we now know, the blade is not attached to anything, so you can't grab something that's not there to grab—not to mention that if there *were* a rope attached, and if you *did* try that, your arms would be wrenched out of their sockets and you'd fail anyway. (Don't forget elementary physics: Things, including guillotine blades, fall rather faster than they often do in dramatic scenes in movies. A guillotine blade takes about half a second to drop fourteen feet. How fast can you grab a swiftly moving rope?)

Nor can your hero, should he be blessed with the world's fastest reflexes, shove a handy stick or pike under the blade to block it before it drops all the way. As we know, the blade with drop-weight weighs about 90 pounds and is falling from a fourteen-foot height. *Nothing* you could shove under it—except possibly a telephone pole or an anvil—is going to stop this thing in its tracks. Try this with something like a two-by-four and the blade is going to smash right through it and *then*, slowed by the obstruction, it's still going to go through the neck beneath it—but at a much slower and much more unpleasant rate of speed.

Even a clumsily managed execution, which happened once or twice during the 19th century under the supervision of drunken executioners, eventually succeeded; nobody ever *survived* a botched guillotining.

Of course, should your hero have a telephone pole or anvil handy to block the blade, go right ahead. I won't stop you.

16

A Grab Bag of Oddments

Cafés and Coffeehouses

 f you want to know what a London coffeehouse or a Paris café was like in the 17th or 18th or even the 19th century, don't waste your money on a trip to Paris in order to visit a touristy café on the Champs-Élysées. For the genuine ambience of an 18th-century café, you'll do better to go to a village coffeehouse in, say, Syria or North Africa or even Greece—but if you're female, be prepared for a lot of hostile stares.

European cafés and English coffeehouses, from the late 1600s well into the 1800s, with a very few exceptions were not in the least like coffee shops or the sort of trendy café you'll find in American cities or college towns today. They didn't serve oversized muffins, or any other kind of food, and were more like gentlemen's social clubs than anything else, where women were not invited and were rarely seen.

Men gathered in cafés and coffeehouses—the regulars, like people at a neighborhood bar, all knew each other well—to escape their wives and families and meet friends, get the latest news, discuss politics, conspire, smoke, conduct business deals, play cards or dice or backgammon or chess, or pick over the latest play or book or scandal that everybody was talking about, all in a highly caffeinated and refreshingly woman-free atmosphere. (The London stock exchange actually began as regular meetings of businessmen in certain 17th-century coffee-houses.) Working-class cafés in continental Europe in the late 18th and early 19th centuries—like the one depicted in *Les Misérables*, patronized by both workers and radical university students—were, moreover, a place where illiterate laborers, both men and women, could hear the news of the day from some-one who would read the newspapers aloud for their benefit.

A French café, first half of the 18th century. The only woman present is the stout lady at left behind the counter, probably the proprietor's wife.

Middle- and upper-class women, meanwhile, stayed at home, the woman's sphere, and served coffee to guests in their own parlors, or visited friends in other parlors. Until late in the 18th century, only women of bad reputation were (occa-sionally) seen in upscale cafés in the company of male friends, probably lovers. In some fashionable cafés, in fact, women were simply forbidden to enter; it's claimed that Fouquet's, the famous Belle Époque café on the Champs-Élysées, did not allow women through its doors until the 20th century.

An English coffeehouse, late 18th century.

By the last quarter of the 18th century, respectable women, escorted by their husbands, might be seen at outdoor tables at cafés located in public parks or gardens. Upper-class women could also now be found at the really high-end, stylish cafés, particularly in Paris after the French Revolution, when social mores were changing and newly-rich, social-climbing women wanted to see and be seen. Café Frascati, founded in 1789, was the most famous of these "family-friendly" cafés, with its elegant interior and pleasant garden; it prided itself on being a glamorous public gathering place where respectable women could go without fear of harassment. But anything could have gone on in the crowded, intimate, masculine atmosphere within a typical 17th- or 18th-century café.

P.S.: Americans: Don't refer to an English coffeehouse of the 17th or 18th century as a "café"; aside from being a foreign term that people of the time wouldn't have used, in Britain today, "café" implies the kind of place that Americans would call a cheap coffee shop or donut shop, in other words a scruffy sort of place with formica tables, where you'd grab a quick bite or a cuppa joe.

Colors

Very few poor people would have been able to wear the brightly colored clothing that they sometimes wear in movies set before the 1850s—or if they did, the colors would soon have faded. Bright, long-lasting aniline (synthetic) dyes were developed in the second half of the 19th century. Before that, cloth was dyed with natural vegetable dyes only, the cheapest of which—primarily dark browns, mossy greens, and brownish reds—were, with a couple of exceptions, more muted and much more easily washed out. We probably all know about "Tyrian purple," the dye from the eastern Mediterranean, produced in tiny quantities from a local mollusk since ancient times, that was so expensive that only royalty could afford it. A few other dyes also produced deep, long-lasting colors, although most of the processes used to produce them were both expensive and revoltingly smelly.

Rich, deep colors were costly and became a sign of high social status from the Middle Ages onward, a trend that only began to fade when a fad for pastels arose in the mid 18th century. Aside from a few natural dyes that leave strong, long-lasting stains (the juice of walnuts' outer husks for brown, for example, or—in Asia—turmeric for yellow), most colors tended to wash out eventually. Ordinary folk, who had to rely on the natural dyes that were cheap and easily available, routinely wore drabber colors than did the rich.

Doorknobs

Americans writing about Europe often get this one wrong. The doorknob, used mostly by the Americans and the English, is an invention that really doesn't make much sense, as a round knob doesn't provide much leverage and people with weak (or very petite) hands or wrists can find them difficult to use. European doors, inside and out, usually have handles (levers to grasp and turn in order to unlatch the door), not knobs; you'll rarely find a doorknob, whether in the 21st century or the 18th. When they do have such things as the decorative round handles frequently found in the middle of street doors in France, they seldom turn like an American doorknob—they are merely stationary knobs to take hold of, not a latch mechanism.

Nobody anywhere had a doorknob before the mid 18th century, and they weren't common in the United States until the 19th century.

Glass vs. Pottery

Glass is a lot more tricky and expensive to make than is pottery, and humans have been making pottery for a lot longer. If it's before the 19th century, unless you're describing a wealthy household, it's likely that any storage vessels, crocks, jars, and so on would have been made of pottery—anything from simple earthenware to brightly glazed chinaware—rather than glass. That includes the big storage jars in apothecary shops, which wouldn't have been likely to be see-through glass until well into the 19th century.

Haves and Have-Nots in the 20th Century

While we, in 2013, can watch a movie made in the 1930s or 40s and feel relatively at home in the setting—after all, the people in them have cars, telephones, radios, and various other modern toys and conveniences—we still have to keep in mind that we're watching something set in Great Depression-era Hollywood Dream Land, where Fred and Ginger are forever dancing in a glittering nightclub. In Hollywood Dream Land, everybody is rich and sophisticated, lives in elegant Art Deco apartments in New York City or Beverly Hills with a couple of sassy maids, and has all the latest toys.

The reality wasn't quite so glamorous. By 1900, 19th-century industrialization and speedily advancing technology had created an ever-widening lifestyle gap between the rich, who could afford every fascinating new invention that would improve one's home and life—water closet, electric lighting, horseless carriage, telephone, phonograph, wireless—as it came along, and the poor, who muddled along without them for years or even decades longer.

Don't be deceived and create your 1920s or 1930s world with the idea that everybody lived like Fred and Ginger. While the One Percent had many of the modern technological conveniences, in some form, that we now take for granted—and the middle classes would aspire to them—the lower middle class and the poor, especially in rural areas, wouldn't have them for many more decades. During World War II, many American soldiers from the farther back of the backwoods had to be taught the rudiments of using electricity and flush toilets when they arrived at boot camp for basic training. Until well into the 1940s at least, the rural poor in America and Europe might still have been living in the middle of the 19th century, for all the access to modern technology they had.

Read Dorothy L. Sayers's *Have His Carcase* (1932) for a memorable portrayal of England's rural south coast in the early 1930s. The glamorous "watering places" (seaside resort towns) are quite up to date and have giant luxury hotels with electric lights, private bathrooms, restaurants, and dance bands; telephones are everywhere; sleek Daimler and Lagonda convertibles are on the streets; and all the comforts and amenities of modern 1930s life are available. The nearby, sparsely settled countryside, however, is still situated firmly in the 1870s or so. While a local train goes by daily, there are far more horses and wagons than cars on the country lanes, the only telephone for miles is in a grocery in a tiny village, and you can be sure that the small farmers' and fishermen's cottages along the coast road have nothing as modern as any kind of running water, electricity, or indoor plumbing.

Rural America was no different. 99% of Americans in the countryside had no access to electric power until FDR's rural electrification bill in the mid 1930s—and even then the percentage rose only to about 25% by the end of the decade.

Remember, the interstate highway system, allowing more commerce as well as more travel, was built only in the 1950s. And although most people in rural areas now have the same computers, satellite TV, and smartphones that urbanites do, until mass communications and media reached far-flung regions in the 1960s, the most modern thing they generally had was the inevitable beat-up old truck or jalopy; Americans in many rural and remote areas, particularly the mountains, were living much as they might have lived in 1920 or before.

Paper

Until the middle of the 19th century, paper, even in daily newspapers, was made mostly of old linen rags and required a complicated, lengthy, and iffy process to manufacture (depending on the weather and the humidity); it was expensive stuff, like all manufactured goods, and treated accordingly. Writing surfaces were even more valuable in the Middle Ages, when papermaking technology was just reaching Europe from China via the Middle East. Medieval paper existed and was fairly widespread, though not cheap, among the literate classes by the 1400s. But the material on which all those monks were creating their gorgeous illuminated manuscripts was usually parchment (treated sheep, calf, or goatskin) or vellum (an extra-fine parchment made of calfskin), which were more expensive than paper but also more durable, and which could be scraped down and re-used if necessary.

Being so valuable, parchment was reserved for fine books and important documents, while paper was used for less treasured books, notebooks, and the accounts and letters of the rich. The author, however, who thoughtlessly gave her young medieval heroine a paper sketching pad to casually doodle on—something that wouldn't exist or be affordable until the 17th or 18th century—badly needed to read up on the technology of the time.

In later centuries, paper began to be produced in greater volume to keep up with the demand created by the invention of the printing press. Any kind of old paper, including newspapers or outdated advertising posters that were stuck on city walls, was eagerly collected by street folk, together with rags, and sold back to paper makers by the pound for recycling. But paper was still expensive and it was never used for "disposable" items until new technologies speeded up the manufacturing process and cheaper high-acid-content, wood-pulp paper began to appear in the 19th century, primarily in newspapers and "penny novels"; it's then that the well-known British tradition of serving greasy fish and chips in yesterday's newspaper was established. But before the introduction of mass-produced, cheaper, flimsier paper, no one except very, very well-off people would have used and wasted paper as casually as we do now.

Pens and pencils

Legendary Hollywood studio head Jack Warner once said to his producers, after a run of period films that flopped, "Don't give me any more pictures where people write with feathers."

Although we tend to think of pencils as modern inventions and pens ("quill pens") as what everyone wrote with in the past, pencils have actually been around for quite a while. The first true pencil was made in Italy in 1560 and pencils were well known, though not terribly common, by the 18th century. Pens were much easier to produce and anyone could make one; they required just a large goose feather (quill) and a small, sharp knife and a few minutes' worth of trimming. Pencils required scarcer components (such as graphite) and many more steps to make, so they were expensive and far less often used than quills until mechanization made cheap mass production possible in the 19th century. But the pencil was still the writing instrument of choice for someone who knew he'd be making a lot of erasures (see Rubber, below) or who needed to carry one about to take notes or write hasty messages—imagine wrestling with a quill and a messy bottle of ink while you're on the go.

And so you don't have someone writing with a ballpoint when they should be using a fountain pen, here's a short history of the modern pen:

Quills are used until the early 19th century, although a few primitive steel pens are known to have existed in the 1700s.

1822: the **steel nib** is introduced and eventually supersedes quills; the steel "dip pen" is used in the same way as a quill, by frequently dipping the point into the ink.

1850s: the **fountain pen** is perfected (with the creation of three elements—improved, non-rusting nibs, hard rubber for the ink reservoirs, and free-flowing ink that won't corrode the reservoir). Fountain pens are mass-produced by the 1880s and become the dominant type of pen.

1938: Laszló Biró, a Hungarian newspaper editor, invents the modern **ballpoint** pen. The ballpoint is gradually perfected in the 1950s and the cheap, portable, disposable ballpoint overtakes the fountain pen for everyday use in the 1960s.

Restaurants

The concept of the *restaurant*—a place to go out to eat and enjoy fine cooking and elegant surroundings—is a relatively new one, dating from the 1790s. Until the "restaurant"—a place to "restore" oneself—was conceived of in mid-18th-century Paris and became fashionable in revolutionary Paris, no one in Europe would have expected to find decent food, let alone fine food, in a public eating-house of any sort.

Until the middle of the 18th century, the rich and aristocratic of Europe employed expert chefs and large kitchen staffs in their households. They dined on fine, elaborate multi-course meals in their own homes or as guests in someone else's home, but wouldn't dream of going to commercial establishments to eat—yuck! (Eating-houses were where *poor* people ate.)

Even middle-class households, depending on their income level, had anything from a full kitchen staff of three or more to—at the lower-middle-class level—at least a half-trained and inexpensive kitchen servant, often an illiterate teenaged peasant girl, to help the mistress of the house with the chores of daily cooking. (See Chapter 14, "Servants.") No one in the middle and upper classes would have gone out to eat and expected to find food better than that served at their own homes.

Prosperous but small households, especially those without a mistress of the house and/or with too few family members to make the keeping of a full-time cook worthwhile, usually used the services of neighborhood caterers, who prepared higher-class and more expensive dishes, along with providing delivery, pickup, and dishwashing. When not dining at friends' homes, which was common—really proficient spongers could often manage to wangle dinner invitations for every day of the week—well-off people who lived alone, such as comfortable bachelors, would have standing orders with a local caterer (*traiteur*) for hot, ready-to-eat fine dinners, which would be delivered to their apartments on covered platters by an errand boy. (Caterers even regularly delivered fancy meals to wealthy people who had landed in prison; no one who could afford to have their dinners sent in was going to touch the standard prison fare.)

Until the late 1700s, eating in a public place was, for the middle and upper classes, strictly for the sake of necessity, usually at roadside inns while traveling. Though inns might try to have one or two upscale entrees available for richer travelers, a really wealthy family would bring its own kitchen staff along on a journey, and send them a few hours ahead to take over kitchens at inns down the road and prepare meals. But eating-houses in cities were strictly for the poor working class who couldn't afford kitchens, such as they were, in their tiny apartments—the cheapest lodgings did not have fireplaces and were heated only with portable charcoal stoves and the like (or with nothing at all). Eating-houses were usually rough, dirty places where you rubbed elbows with others along benches and ate cheap bad food of very dubious provenance—essentially the equivalent of the modern greasy-spoon diner with the $1.99 breakfast special.

A famous Parisian restaurant, *Les Trois Frères Provençeaux*, in 1842. Ladies are present, though always escorted by a gentleman.

The concept of the *restaurant*, on the other hand—an elegant, expensive establishment serving elegant, expensive food, where the fashionable and famous went out to dine—took off in the early 1790s in Paris, in the first years of the French Revolution. The newly unemployed top-of-the-line private chefs of the former nobility (many of whom had emigrated) needed to create work for themselves somehow, and the new power and new celebrities of the time—revolutionary leaders, mostly from the middle class—wanted to mingle and be seen.

By 1793 there were a few of what we'd think of as fashionable restaurants in Paris, in which prominent revolutionaries often gathered to dine, mixing with the usual theater and opera stars and the newly rich financiers, war profiteers, and the like. By the time the old nobility returned to power in Europe twenty-five years later, after the fall of Napoleon, public dining in elegant restaurants had become so entrenched a custom that eventually even the nobility gave in to what was rather a tacky, *nouveau riche* practice of eating in public— something the prerevolutionary aristocracy would never have dreamed of doing.

Rubber and elastic

Rubber, you'll recall if you paid attention in Chapter 6 ("Food, Plants, & Animals"), originally came from South America. (Don't let the term "India rubber," which was tacked onto it during the 19th century, after the British started up rubber plantations throughout South Asia, fool you!) It was introduced to Europe in the middle of the 18th century and slowly made its way through the continent as a curious new product for another hundred years.

Its natural properties, however (it charred or melted too easily, and was too stiff when cold and too soft when warmed), kept it from being of much commercial use beyond that of "rubbing out" pencil marks (hence the word "rubber") until Charles Goodyear invented vulcanization in 1839. The process of vulcanization, in which hardening chemicals are added to heated rubber, keeps rubber from perishing and made it much, much more useful for many industrial and commercial purposes—most modern industries and technologies couldn't have begun without it. So don't give rubber a major presence in HF, beyond acting as an eraser, before the 1850s or so— and don't give anybody any kind of elastics in their clothing for at least another few decades after that.

(And in case you were wondering, the first rubber condom was made in 1855, and was about as thick as the rubber skin of a bicycle's inner tube. Latex, thank goodness, was invented in 1920.)

Stirrups

The most glaring horse-related anachronism found in HF (and movies) is probably the sight of Romans, and other ancient Mediterranean or Middle Eastern peoples, using saddles with stirrups.

The modern stirrup is by far the most important thing that allows people of moderate strength, and who are only average riders, to stay on top of the moving mountain that is a horse. People like the Asian barbarian tribes or American Plains Indians, who rode bareback, or just rode on top of some kind of stirrupless light saddle or pad and hooked their feet into the saddle girth, had to be magnificent riders with very, very strong legs in order to stay on. So you'd think that such a mind-bogglingly useful and relatively simple invention as the stirrup would have been around forever—that the ancient Babylonians or Egyptians probably came up with it. Not the case. The saddle with stirrups only appeared in the West in the Dark Ages—around A.D. 600, probably adopted from invading barbarians who had adopted it from the Chinese.

While plenty of sword-and-sandal movies tend to have ancient Romans riding with modern stirrups, no Roman of the Republic or the Empire ever did—nor did the ancient Sumerians, Greeks, Egyptians (who preferred their horses to be drawing chariots anyway), or Romano-British chieftains—the real King Arthur's mounted troops of the late 5th century would have been riding without stirrups, too. Keep your ancient characters out of them.

Telephones

Paradoxically, many familiar modern machines and labor-saving conveniences were invented and in use quite a bit earlier than we'd think. The telephone was patented by Alexander Graham Bell in 1876 and the first telephone exchange, in New Haven, Connecticut, was set up in 1878. Phones were in regular use in cities, on both sides of the Atlantic, by businesses (like the production office of Gilbert and Sullivan's Savoy Theatre) and wealthy private individuals in the early 1880s.

However, this hasn't prevented authors from putting the wrong kind of technology in the wrong time; the author who knew that well-off people had telephones in 1912 still hadn't quite grasped the fact that the very first *dial* telephones only made their appearance in 1919. (At right: a telephone from 1896, with hand crank to power it up so you could reach the operator—but no dial.)

Until 1919 at the earliest, and until at least a decade later in most areas, you made all your calls through the operator ("the Exchange" in Britain), by picking up the earpiece or handset from the cradle, waiting for an operator to say "What number, please?", and reciting the number you wished to call; the operator would then manually connect you at the switchboard. Rotary dial telephones made it possible to reach the number you were calling without going through an operator, but direct dialing could be used only for local calls. Though direct dial service began in 1919, it did not become common until the late 1920s and early 30s.[32] And the last manual (solely switchboard-operated) telephone systems in the U.S. Bell System were not converted to direct dial until . . . wait for it . . . 1978.

The rotary dial on the "basic black" AT&T-issue phone

---

[32] Visit http://www.corp.att.com/history/other/sounds.wmv to watch a one-minute informational film that the phone company used in the 1930s to tell people how to use their new direct-dial service. More telephone history at http://www.corp.att.com/history/milestones.html .

was *nearly* universal from the 1930s through the 1970s (the first Touch-Tone phone appeared in 1963), and stuck around even into the 80s and 90s for those who weren't ready to spend money on a fancy new push-button phone just yet.

A long-distance call couldn't be dialed directly; you still had to set up long-distance calls through the long-distance operator well into the 1950s. If your call was to a distant destination, it might go through several linked exchanges and take ten or fifteen minutes to set up; usually the operator would offer to call you back to let you know when your call was ready. And those of us born before 1980 or so can remember that until the 1990s, if you were on a tight budget, you kept your long-distance and international calls to an absolute minimum and didn't chatter for hours on end to friends on the other side of the country or relatives on other continents. Although they were all direct-dialed by the late 70s, long-distance calls used to be shockingly expensive per minute[33] before AT&T's monopoly was broken up in the early 80s and the "unlimited long distance" monthly plan was born some time later.

And does anybody remember party lines?

Nearly everyone had one in the 1930s and 40s, when phone service came to an area through a single line and then was split between several local customers. Everyone's phone rang every time a call came through for anyone on the party line, and each household had its own distinctive ring (two long, one short; one long, two short, etc.) so they could tell if the call was for them or not. It was considered bad form to pick up your handset and listen in on your neighbors' conversations, although plenty of nosy people did: Overhearing a disturbing conversation on a party line was the basis of at least one mystery novel of the era.

---

[33] Though at least the price came down somewhat from the early days of long distance calling. According to AT&T, cross-country long-distance service was available to all telephone customers by 1915, "but at an initial price of $20.70 for the first three minutes between New York and San Francisco, volume is low." No wonder—that's about $400 in 2013 money.

Party lines were commonest in the 30s and 40s, but they stuck around, in a slightly improved form (when a call came in, the phone only rang on the intended recipient's line, but you might pick up the phone to make a call and find that the line was already occupied) for a long time after that in rural areas. They were still common in not-so-far-upstate New York until the late 1980s, when I had one myself.

Window Screens

Insect screens were invented in the 1820s and you won't be committing an anachronism if you put them in mid-19th-century American windows. (Screen doors are a later invention, and weren't common before 1900.)

Most Europeans, however, not being plagued with mosquitoes and gnats as North Americans are, simply don't need or use screens, even today. Don't thoughtlessly put screens in European windows, no matter what century it is!

17

And Finally, the End: Death & Burial

The modern Western funeral industry has lined its own nest pretty well for the past 150 years or so by convincing us that "only the best will do for our loved ones" and that everybody, no matter how undistinguished his/her life, deserves and needs to have lots of money spent on him/her in death for a perfectly embalmed corpse, an expensive funeral with lots of flowers, a fancy casket (a commercial euphemism for the grimmer-sounding "coffin"—see below), a permanent, individual grave plot in a pretty cemetery, and a massive headstone (a.k.a. a "memorial," which sounds so much more impressive and sentimental). But if you have the vague idea that this must have been the case for everyone for most of Western history, and you are tempted to write about a 17th-century peasant's widow weeping beside her late husband's headstone ten years later, then you need to shake off the funeral industry's brainwashing and take a look at actual European burial customs for the greater part of the past couple of thousand years.

Strict Christian religious custom really only requires that the deceased be buried in consecrated ground (or in a consecrated space such as a church's crypt), with a priest in attendance to recite the offices for the dead and sanctify the proceedings. Period, the end. Nowhere in the Bible or in traditional Catholic or Protestant doctrine does it say anything about caskets, flowers, "memorials," or a need for an individual, permanent burial spot.

A Christian peasant or poor urban laborer anywhere in Europe for the past two thousand years, until well into the 19th century, didn't expect his final "resting place" to be either pretty, sentimental, or undisturbed. He expected only to be quickly buried, without a marker, in holy ground—which was the sole important issue in how his remains were disposed of, because it was important to the fate of his soul. The trappings, the fancy treatment of the flesh—the corpse—were pretty much an unaffordable luxury and entirely beside the point to the faithful Christian unless he was a member of the elite.

Coffins and tombstones? Expensive and out of the question—the cost far, far beyond the reach of the average laborer or peasant who was barely able to buy food and pay his rent or taxes; the vast majority couldn't even afford to bury their dead in their clothes, much less spend money on a coffin. Individual, permanent grave plots? Only for kings and princes, the rich and nobly-born, who had performed notable deeds (at least in their own opinion) that might be chiseled on a stone monument for posterity, in which case they would be granted space for a fancy tomb somewhere inside an important or favored church. The famous, such as artists and writers, whose fame was greater than their fortunes often were buried very modestly until their devoted students, protégés, and fans could raise enough money to build an elaborate monument.

The average 12th- or 15th- or 18th-century European town dweller, the poor, subsistence-level, working-class, unexceptional "Joe Sixpack" of medieval, Renaissance, or Enlightenment Europe, on the other hand, knew quite well what was going to happen after his death. He expected his corpse to be "laid out," washed, and wrapped inside a shroud or "winding sheet," essentially a coarse cloth sack, enveloping the naked body: In ages when all clothing was hand-spun, hand-woven, and hand-sewn, it was much too valuable to be buried with the dead.[34]

He'd be laid in a mass grave next to a church—essentially a sanctified garbage dump for the bodies of the poor—together with dozens of other recently deceased bodies of his equally poor neighbors, with a few inches of soil separating the layers of corpses in what could be a twenty- or thirty-foot-deep pit. (We know about medieval "plague pits" that have been excavated recently in London and elsewhere, but the fact is that such burial trenches were routine for the period. They simply filled up a lot faster, and more trenches were required, during deadly epidemics. The archaeological evidence, however, proves to us that even the plague corpses were not just hurriedly dumped in and covered up; the bodies still seem to have received some consideration, for the skeletons, for the most part, were found arranged in rows.)

Our medieval Joe Sixpack also knew that in five or ten or twenty years, when the churchyard's grounds were full up, urban space in crowded European cities being at a premium, the oldest common grave would be dug up. All the surviving bones would be collected and stored together—probably in an underground ossuary or bone crypt beneath the church; or in an above-ground gallery, called a "charnel," surrounding the burial enclosure—and the trench reused. The trenches were used over and over again, sometimes for centuries—individualizing remains or a grave site of a "nobody" was completely irrelevant. The deceased's relatives knew that their loved one's bones were somewhere within the church's sanctified grounds and that was all that really mattered; praying for the family member's soul or having a Mass said for the dead was far more important than visiting physical remains at a gravesite.

---

[34] Richard Cobb's *Death in Paris* (Oxford University Press, 1978) describes the morgue where suicides or accident victims found in the Seine were brought in the 1790s. Many of the relatives who came to identify corpses would claim the clothes, which could be reused or sold, but leave the body behind, to be buried at the city's expense in the paupers' mass graves.

Much the same process still goes on in municipal "potter's fields," the largest being New York City's Hart Island burial ground, where unidentified or unclaimed bodies are buried in mass graves similar to medieval Europe's trenches—though each corpse, in case it needs to be located and exhumed within the next few years, does receive a plain, numbered pine box at the taxpayers' expense. Until quite recently, the burial trenches were continually re-excavated and reused every twenty-five years or so; between 700,000 and one million bodies have been interred on Hart Island since the 1850s.

While a medieval or Renaissance peasant in a small village might have had an individual grave dug in the churchyard at the time of his death, because there weren't enough burials in rural areas at any given time, except during plagues, to justify a mass trench, ordinary people's plots were not "owned" or private or permanent in any way and rarely were marked with much more than a crude wooden cross. The peasant fully expected that the anonymous spot where his corpse lay would be dug up sooner or later, and his bones shoved aside (but still within holy ground) in order to make way for a new burial of someone equally anonymous.

Reread the classic graveyard scene in *Hamlet* to get an idea of how matter-of-fact this process of constantly reusing cemetery ground was. While digging Ophelia's grave, the gravediggers casually come across old bones, comment on them, toss them around, make jokes about them, and will eventually rebury them or carry them to an ossuary. The consecrated ground is important; the identification of the bones is not.

The most famous example of the endless reuse of burial land is in Paris. The bones of six million Parisians from the 13th to the early 19th centuries are now stored eight stories below ground level, in ancient disused limestone quarries that were officially consecrated for Catholic burials in 1786. These are the "Catacombes," a.k.a. the Municipal Ossuary of Paris, where you can gape at the bizarre arrangements of skulls and thighbones, as well as at the mind-blowing *quantity* of human bones that are piled five or six feet high in a solid mass, filling underground chambers that sometimes go back thirty or forty feet.

All those millions of bones were once buried in dozens of medieval churchyards around the city, in mass graves that were constantly reused for up to six centuries. The custom only came to a halt when Paris's growth and volume of burials became so great in the 1780s that the stink threatened to asphyxiate neighborhoods near the Cemetery of the Holy Innocents, the largest and oldest of the burial grounds (now the innocuous Place Joachim du Bellay in central Paris).

Even Père-Lachaise, the new and "modern" cemetery inaugurated in 1802 at what was then the outskirts of Paris, at first had a large portion of its space reserved for mass burials of the poorer classes who couldn't afford a permanent grave plot, under the assumption that burial customs would continue in much the same fashion as they always had. As the 19th century saw the rise of the wealthy middle class, however, the very new and bourgeois concept of a "concession in perpetuity"—*buying* a permanent plot in a commercially run burying ground for the individual or the family, rather than being granted space for a tomb or a family chapel in a church because of one's aristocratic blood or historic deeds or financial contributions to the parish—quickly caught on.

What's more, the Enlightenment and the French Revolution had spawned all sorts of new concepts of individualism and secularism, including the startling idea that holy ground wasn't the *only* important thing—displaying one's wealth via the elaborate family tomb was nice, too—and that unmarked mass graves were unacceptable for anyone but the completely destitute. By the middle of the 19th century, demand for individual concessions had risen so much that the mass graves at Père-Lachaise were excavated (the bones sent to the Catacombes, naturally) and the reclaimed acreage sold or leased out as private plots. The cemetery—despite two major enlargements—was filled to capacity by the mid 20th century.

So, should you be thinking of having yourself buried in Paris, there's a very, very long waiting list for those high-priced plots that now and then come on the market.[35] But they no longer sell permanent concessions at Père-Lachaise; grave sites there are now offered in 30-year or 50-year leases only . . . and if a family doesn't renew the lease at the end of the term, or if the cemetery officials choose not to allow the lease to be renewed, the plot is excavated and the remains are returned to the family, if they're still around, or are labeled and stored in the cemetery's ossuary, in order to re-use the coveted space.

Perhaps things haven't changed so much, after all.

Aside: So what exactly is the difference between a coffin and a casket?

Strictly speaking, any container made to hold a dead human body is a coffin; while the word "casket" began its existence in the Middle Ages when it had nothing to do with corpses, but meant an ornamental box or chest, small enough to be carried easily by one person, that held small valuables such as jewelry or spices. The American funeral industry, in the late 19th century, latched on to the word as a genteel euphemism to refer to coffins of any shape—so don't use an anachronistic term by writing about wealthy 16th-century mourners gathering around a departed character's "casket."

In general funeral industry jargon today, a "coffin" is the item on the next page, the classic, relatively plain, flat-topped wooden box with six sides that is widest at the shoulders and

[35] You also need to have been born in Paris, or to have lived in Paris for a certain length of time, or to have died in Paris.

tapers toward the feet; while a "casket" is a rectangular box, often with a split lid to allow for viewing of the deceased, and is usually more ornate than a simple coffin. The classic six-sided "coffin" shape has been around for a few centuries

and was overtaken in popularity by the rectangular "casket"—which first appeared in the USA in the late 1800s—only in the 20th century.

The stone sarcophagi of early medieval royalty and notables had four sides but often were a trapezoidal wedge shape rather than rectangular—the coffin was slightly wider at the head end than at the foot end. Medieval and Early Modern wooden or lead coffins sometimes used this shape as well, until the six-sided shape became more popular in the 18th century. A genuine 14th-century coffin can be seen today, set bizarrely into the open-air ruins of St. John's Church in Chester, England. "The coffin in the wall" was shaped from a single solid tree trunk into an approximation of the usual trapezoidal shape, allowing for the not quite straight lines of the original trunk, although its interior was carved out to roughly form-fit the body it would hold, including a round space for the head.[36]

---

[36] Wikimedia Commons has a good photo: http://commons.wikimedia.org/wiki/File:St_John%27s_Church,_Chester_-_Ruine_2_Sarg.jpg

Medieval depiction of "the dance of death" worthy of a horror movie: Only the two cavorting figures in the center are completely skeletonized—the other three corpses are still decomposing and spilling their innards as they emerge from the graveyard. Note that the corpses are draped in their decaying "winding sheets" but are otherwise naked.

18

Bibliography & Research: Further Reading

o, now that we know about the really big honking mistakes we should never make in our HF, where do we find all the information we need in order not to make all the other, smaller, silly mistakes, and find the right information for the specific time and place we're researching?

As I've mentioned before, the Internet is the simplest, quickest, and most accessible source for plain facts—the unambiguous yes-or-no answers to the "Are dandelions native to North America?" and "Did ancient Egyptians wear cotton?" kind of questions. If you need to find out or confirm a basic detail of life in the past, the Net will usually have it for you somewhere.

But don't forget the library! If you are lucky enough to live in a college town or a medium-sized or large city, your local public library or—even better—university library is a priceless asset for your historical research, especially when you're reading in depth, studying the major events, personalities, and mindsets of a period and not just the little details of everyday life.

Try the following books, suggested by a librarian, to help

you get started in major research libraries (though they are geared more toward academic and scientific writers than to writers of HF):

Mann, Thomas. *The Oxford Guide to Library Research, 3rd Edition*. Oxford University Press, 2005 [paper and eBook]

Booth, Wayne C., Colomb, Gregory G., & Williams, Joseph M. *The Craft of Research, Third Edition* (Chicago Guides to Writing, Editing, and Publishing). University of Chicago Press, 2008. [paper and eBook]

Hartman, Karen, & Ackermann, Ernest. *Searching and Researching on the Internet and the World Wide Web, 5th Edition*. Franklin, Beedle & Associates Inc., 2010. [ironically, paper only]

HF writers who don't have access to giant university libraries or large urban library systems will still find many books about daily life in past ages in their local public libraries, and they're usually a lot of fun to read—you'll painlessly pick up all sorts of useful information about the period you're interested in. The librarians at the information or reference desk can help you if you don't know where to start; or you can amuse yourself at the computerized catalogue by inputting some keywords—you never know what the catalogue may come up with, perhaps some weird, wonderful, inconceivably useful book that you never dreamed existed.

Nearly any work of nonfiction with a title like *Daily Life in* _____ (enter your period of interest here) will be a help with details for the HF writer. A long series of books with these titles, covering the past few thousand years across the globe, originally published in France in the 1960s, were published in English translation in the 60s and 70s and are excellent resources. Time-Life Books, in the 1990s, published a heavily illustrated, full-color series of coffee-table books called *What Life Was Like* (see incomplete list below). These are also great sources for background information.

If you intend to build up a research library of your own, my favorite, and the most comprehensive, source for buying out-of-print, used, or obscure books all over the world is bookfinder.com, which searches major bookselling networks worldwide, including ABE, Amazon, and networks of European book dealers. Give it a try by entering "daily life" or "everyday life" in the "title" search box—hundreds of titles will come up.

If you have an e-reader of some kind (or are willing to read eBooks on your computer screen), not-for-profit Project Gutenberg (gutenberg.org) has the searchable texts of thousands of out-of-copyright books published before 1923 available as free downloads in various formats, including pdf, Kindle, plain text, and more. These include such unlikely research treasures, for those interested in Victoriana, as 19th-century cookbooks and books on household management; for writers studying earlier periods, there are many, many period memoirs, autobiographies, and history books from the 18th, 19th, and early 20th centuries. While they are not always as detailed or reliable as more recent works, a 19th-century overview of a period can get you started and help you focus on what you find most interesting.

Another fabulous source of online books is Google Books (books.google.com/advanced_book_search), a virtual archive of millions of complete scans of long-out-of-copyright books and bound collections of newspapers, magazines, and journals from major research libraries. Google Books allows you to download entire out-of-copyright book files in PDF or, sometimes, EPUB format, without charge (to get free, fully downloadable books, choose "Full view only" or "Google eBooks only" when you're defining your search). Depending on the age of the books and the clarity of the typefaces, sometimes their texts are even searchable—if you're looking for a specific name, for example, try searching text within book files by using the search boxes in the pale blue area at the top of your screen.

Here's a relatively short list of random books on details of everyday life in past centuries—some from my own collection and many of which supplied facts mentioned in this book—to get you started in the library catalogue and give you an idea of the variety of material that is out there:

General:

Ariès, Philippe, general editor. *A History of Private Life* series, 5 volumes: *I: From Pagan Rome to Byzantium*; *II: Revelations of the Medieval World*; *III: Passions of the Renaissance*; *IV: From the Fires of Revolution to the Great War*; *V: Riddles of Identity in Modern Times*. Cambridge, MA: Harvard/Belknap Press, 1987-1994.

Ariès, Philippe. *The Hour of our Death: A Classic History of Western Attitudes Toward Death Over the Last One Thousand Years*. NY: Knopf, 1981.

Andersen, Christopher P. *The Name Game*. NY: Simon & Schuster, 1977.

Ball, Krista D. *What Kings Ate and Wizards Drank*. Tyche Books, 2012 (eBook; paperback 2013). [A guide to help anchor authors of heroic fantasy in historically realistic daily life (how do you catch, cook, and/or preserve the food you're taking along on your quest for the Magic Thingamabob when you live in a preindustrial society?); excellent for authors of historical adventure, too.]

Clark, David P. *Germs, Genes, & Civilization: How Epidemics Shaped Who We Are Today*. FT Press, 2010.

Fletcher, Nichola. *Charlemagne's Tablecloth: A Piquant History of Feasting*. NY; St. Martin's Press, 2004.

Foster, Nelson, & Linda S. Cordell. *Chilies to Chocolate: Food the Americas Gave the World*. Phoenix, AZ: University of Arizona Press, 1992.

Harrold, Chris, & Fletcher Watkins. *The Cigarette Book: The History & Culture of Smoking*. NY: Skyhorse, 2010.

Hartink, A. E. *The Complete Encyclopedia of Antique Firearms: An Expert Guide to Firearms and Their Development*. Hackberry Press, 2001.

Panati, Charles. *Extraordinary Origins of Everyday Things*. NY: William Morrow, 1989.

Panati, Charles. *Extraordinary Endings of Practically Everything and Everybody*. NY: HarperCollins, 1989. [Panati has written several other useful books on the origins of common things and ideas]

Prentice, E. Parmalee. *Hunger and History: The influence of hunger on human history*. Caldwell, ID: Caxton, 1951. [History of food production, famines, & the results throughout history since ancient times]

Quennell, Marjorie & C.H.B. *A History of Everyday Things in England:* [Five volumes] *Part 1: 1066-1499. Part 2: 1500-1799. Part 3: 1733-1851. Part 4: 1851-1914. Part 5: 1914-1968*. London: Batsford, many editions and reprints.

Readers Digest editors. *How Was it Done? The Story of Human Ingenuity Through the Ages*. London: Readers Digest Association Ltd., 1995.

Smith, Elsdon C. *Treasury of Name Lore*. NY: Harper & Row, 1967.

Time-Life Books editors. *What Life was Like at the Dawn of Democracy: Classical Athens, 525-322 B.C.* Alexandria, VA; Time-Life Books, 1997. [and many other titles in the "What Life Was Like" series: *Among Druids And High Kings (Celtic Ireland AD 400-1200); When Rome Ruled the World (The Roman Empire 100 BC-AD 200); Among Samurai and Shoguns (Japan, AD 1000-1700); In the Jewel in the Crown (British India, 1600-1905); During the Age of Reason (France AD 1660-1800); When the Longships Sailed (Vikings AD 800-1100); In the Lands of the Prophet (the Islamic World, AD 570-1405)* . . . and many more!]

Wilson, Bee. *Consider the Fork: A History of How We Cook and Eat*. NY: Basic Books, 2012.

Ancient:

Carcopino, Jerome. *Daily Life in Ancient Rome: The People and the City at the Height of the Empire*. New Haven, CT: Yale University Press, 1940.

Carpenter, Rhys, et al (*National Geographic* eds.). *Everyday Life in Ancient Times: Highlights of the Beginnings of Western Civilization in Mesopotamia, Egypt, Greece, and Rome*. Washington, DC: National Geographic Society, 1951.

Flacelière, Robert. *Daily Life in Greece at the Time of Pericles*. London: Weidenfeld & Nicolson, 1965.

Mireaux, Emile. *Daily Life in the Time of Homer*. NY: Macmillan, 1959.

National Geographic eds. *Everyday Life in Bible Times*. Washington, DC: National Geographic Society, 1969.

Packer, James I., & M.C. Tenney & W. White, jr, eds. *Everyday Life in the Bible: The Old and New Testaments*. Bonanza Books, double edition copyright 1989.

Quennell, Marjorie & C.H.B. *Everyday Life in Prehistoric Times*. NY: Putnam, 1959.

Dark Ages/Middle Ages, to ca. 1400:

Burke, John. *Life in the Castle in Medieval England*. British Heritage Press, 1986.

Davis, William Stearns. *Life on a Mediaeval Barony: A Picture of a Typical Feudal Community in the Thirteenth Century*. NY: Harper & Bros, 1923.

Gies, Joseph & Frances. *Life in a Medieval Castle*. NY: Harper & Row, 1974.

Lacey, Robert, & Danny Danziger. *The Year 1000: What life was like at the turn of the first millennium—An Englishman's world*. Boston: Little, Brown, 1999.

Newman, Paul B. *Daily Life in the Middle Ages*. McFarland, 2001. (reprint; also eBook)

Renaissance/Tudor era, 1400-1600:

Burton, Elizabeth. *The Pageant of Early Tudor England*. Charles Scribner's Sons, 1967. [Burton also wrote at least four other books in the series, *The Pageant of Elizabethan England; Stuart England; Georgian England; Early Victorian England*]

Chamberlin, E.R. *Everyday Life in Renaissance Times*. NY: Capricorn, 1967.

Chancellor, E. Beresford. *The Pleasure Haunts of London During Four Centuries*. Boston: Houghton Mifflin, 1925.

Mountfield, David. *Everyday Life in Elizabethan England*. Editions Minerva, 1978.

Early Modern, 1600-1750:

Bradby, G.F. *The Great Days of Versailles: Studies From Court Life in the Later Years of Louis XIV*. NY: Scribners, 1906.

Carr, John Laurence. *Life in France Under Louis XIV*. NY: Capricorn, 1970.

Earle, Alice Morse. *Child Life in Colonial Days*. Williamstown, MA: Corner House Publications, 1984.

Hole, Christina. *English Home-Life, 1500 to 1800*. London; Batsford, 1949.

Hugon, Cecile. *Social France in the XVII Century*. NY: Macmillan, 1911. [Daily life of the wealthy, aristocratic, & royal in 17th-century France.]

Levron, Jacques. *Daily Life at Versailles in the seventeenth and eighteenth centuries*. Macmillan, 1968.

Marshall, Rosalind K. *The Days of Duchess Anne: Life in the Household of the Duchess of Hamilton, 1656-1716*. NY: St Martin's, 1973.

Orleans, Elisabeth-Charlotte, duchesse d'. *A Woman's Life in the Court of the Sun King: Letters of Liselotte von der Pfalz, Elisabeth Charlotte, Duchesse d'Orleans, 1652-1722*. Johns Hopkins University Press, 1984.

Roche, Daniel. *A History of Everyday Things: The Birth of Consumption in France, 1600-1800*. Cambridge University Press, 2000.

Thomson, Gladys Scott. *Life in a Noble Household, 1641-1700*. University of Michigan Press, 1936.

Williams, Guy. *The Age of Agony: The Art of Healing, 1700-1800*. Academy Chicago, 1986. [medicine and medical practices in 18th-century England and Europe]

Zumthor, Paul. *Daily Life in Rembrandt's Holland*. NY: Macmillan, 1963.

Industrial Revolution/Modern, 1750-2000:

Allen, Rick. *The Moving Pageant: A Literary Sourcebook on London Street-Life, 1700-1914*. London: Routledge, 1998.

Ashton, John. *When William IV Was King*. D. Appleton & Company, 1896. [England in the 1830s]

Barbeau, A. *Life and Letters at Bath in the XVIIIth Century*. London: William Heinemann, 1904.

Bernier, Olivier. *Pleasure and Privilege: Life in France, Naples and America 1770-1790*. Garden City, NY: Doubleday, 1981.

Brion, Marcel. *Daily Life in the Vienna of Mozart and Schubert*. NY: Macmillan, 1962.

Ducros, Louis. *French Society in the 18th Century*. G. P. Putnam's Sons, 1927.

Engelmann, Bernt. *In Hitler's Germany: Everyday Life in the Third Reich*. NY: Pantheon, 1986.

Garrioch, David. *The Making of Revolutionary Paris*. University of California Press, 2004.

George, M. Dorothy. *London Life in the Eighteenth Century*. NY: Capricorn, 1965.

Girouard, Mark. *Life in the English Country House*. NY: Penguin Books, 1980.

Guillaumin, Emile. *The Life of a Simple Man*. University Press of New England, 1983. [Classic, semi-fictional account of a 19th-century French peasant farmer's life.]

Hart, Roger. *English Life in the Eighteenth Century*. NY: Putnam, 1970.

Hughes, Kristine. *The Writer's Guide to Everyday Life in Regency & Victorian England, 1811-1901*. Writer's Digest Books, 1998. [Many similar books—*The Writer's Guide to Everyday Life in _____*— were also published by WD Books in the 1990s.]

Jacobs, Marc & Peter Scholliers. *Eating Out in Europe: Picnics, Gourmet Dining & Snacks since the Late Eighteenth Century*. Berg Publications, 2003.

Larkin, Jack. *The Reshaping of Everyday Life: 1790-1840*. NY: Harper & Row, 1988. [America and Americans in the first decades of the republic.]

Laver, James. *The Age of Illusion: Manners and Morals 1750-1848*. D. McKay Co, 1972.

Legge, J.G. *Rhyme and Revolution in Germany: A Study in German History, Life, Literature, and Character, 1813-1850*. London; Constable, 1918.

Lewis, Gwynne. *Life in Revolutionary France*. Putnam, 1972.

Lofts, Norah. *Domestic Life in England*. London: Weidenfeld & Nicolson, 1976.

Marshall, Dorothy. *English People in the Eighteenth Century*. London: Longmans, Green, 1956.

McCutcheon, Marc. *The Writer's Guide to Everyday Life in the 1800s*. Writer's Digest Books, 1993. [19th-century America]

Pool, Daniel. *What Jane Austen Ate and Charles Dickens Knew: From Fox Hunting to Whist—the Facts of Daily Life in Nineteenth-Century England*. NY: Simon & Schuster, 1993.

Rice, Howard C., Jr. *Thomas Jefferson's Paris*. Princeton University Press, 1976.

Sutherland, John. *Is Heathcliff a Murderer? Puzzles in 19th-century Fiction; Can Jane Eyre Be Happy? More Puzzles in Classic Fiction; Who Betrays Elizabeth Bennet? Further Puzzles in Classic Fiction*. Oxford University Press, 1996-1999. [3 collections of essays discussing unresolved puzzles, hidden issues, and anachronisms in classic English and American literature of the 18th and 19th centuries, and touching on many matters of daily life in those periods—including toilets and teeth—as reflected in the literature.]

Thompson, C.J.S. *Love, Marriage and Romance in Old London*. Heath Cranton, 1936.

Afterword

riters and readers: Do you have a pet peeve of your own about an error or anachronism, major or minor, that frequently appears in your favorite historical fiction, or a suggestion for a topic? Would you like to share the worst or funniest anachronism or howler that's brought you to a screeching halt in the course of your reading?

Email me via my website, www.susannealleyn.com, with suggestions or—oh noooo!—possible corrections of any errors I've committed myself. I'd love to hear your ideas and I may be able to tackle them in a future edition of *Medieval Underpants*.

I wish you the best of luck with your historical research.

Now go and *write*!

Reader reviews of books are becoming more important than ever to authors' careers. If you enjoyed this book, please recommend it to your fellow history lovers—and please consider leaving a review, or starting a discussion, at Amazon.com, Goodreads, LibraryThing, or at a book forum or history or historical fiction discussion group to get the word out to other readers who might enjoy it as well.

Would your local book club, class, or writers' group like to discuss *Medieval Underpants and Other Blunders* or any of my novels? Visit my author website, www.susannealleyn. com, for suggestions for discussion topics, or to contact me and schedule a live chat with your group (in the United States, Canada, or the UK), in person or via your speakerphone. I look forward to our conversation.

Thank you in advance,
Susanne Alleyn

About the Author

Susanne Alleyn has loved history all her life, aided and abetted by her grandmother, Lillie V. Albrecht, an author of historical children's books in the 1950s and 60s. (Susanne is delighted to make Mrs. Albrecht's books available again through the magic of eBooks and Print on Demand.) Happy to describe herself as an insufferable knowitall about historical trivia (although she lost on *Jeopardy!*), Susanne has been writing and researching historical fiction for nearly three decades. Her sixth novel, *The Executioner's Heir*, first in a pair of novels about eighteenth-century Parisian executioner Charles Sanson, is now in print. Read more, or send Susanne e-mail, at www. susannealleyn.com.

Read on to sample the first chapter of *The Executioner's Heir*.

The Executioner's Heir

1

April 1753

Paris

"This is the sword of justice," Jean-Baptiste told him, lifting it from its long, straw-lined, padlocked crate. "It first belonged to your great-grandfather."

Great-grandfather—the first Charles Sanson in the profession, the first to hold the Paris title, *Master of High Works for the City and Provostry of Paris and Versailles*. His sword was a family heirloom, of sorts, Charles knew, but the kind you didn't boast about.

Engraved near the two-handed hilt, the single word *Iustitia*—Justice—glinted in the light. The gentle spring sunshine spilled through the door into the shadows of the windowless shed, giving murky outlines to other, less graceful objects: coils of rope, oaken planks, leather whips, a brazier, an iron cudgel, a cart wheel.

The sword was three and a half feet long, with a fine, narrow blade kept oiled and gleaming. It was a beautiful thing, if you could manage to forget what it was meant for.

"Go on, take it," his father said. Charles guessed what he'd left unspoken: *You'll have to lift it one day.*

"It's heavy!"

"It has to be. You've been looking through the *Treatise on the Human Skeleton*—don't you remember what neck bones look like? Slicing through them isn't easy."

"No, Father." He balanced the sword in his hands, the point upward, wondering how much it weighed and if his forefathers had found it as intimidating as he did. He would far rather have been back in Jean-Baptiste's library, leafing through the medical and scientific books that his father, his grandfather Charles Sanson the Second, and great-grandfather Charles Sanson the First had collected over the past sixty or seventy years.

"Charles, have you any idea how one beheads a man with a sword?"

The question, almost matter-of-fact, quietly asked, jerked him back to the present. He glanced up at his father, who gazed at him, unsmiling as always.

"You're fourteen now, old enough. You'll have to learn."

"I…" Occasionally—before his stepmother hurried him away—he caught sight of Jean-Baptiste practicing with a sword, or a facsimile of one, in a yard well away from the house, beyond the stable where he kept the horses and cart that transported criminals to execution at the Place de Grève. But his father was merely aiming at a standing post or at bundles of straw, a harmless enough pastime, you'd think.

"I suppose you lift it up in the air," he said, groping for words, "and—and chop down—like chopping firewood."

"No," Jean-Baptiste said, taking back the weapon, which Charles willingly relinquished to him. "That's not how it's done. Chopping with an axe on a block—that's a clumsy method. Crude."

No doubt his father expected him to show some respectful, though not unseemly, curiosity about the family profession.

"How do you do it, then?"

"You have to swing it sideways."

"Sideways?"

"Like this." Jean-Baptiste gripped the long hilt in both hands, raised the sword almost to shoulder height and parallel to the ground, and slowly described a wide, horizontal arc at arm's length. The steel glittered, flashing in Charles's eyes, as it swept past.

"The patient kneels in front of you, upright, with his back to you."

Patient?

Charles stifled an uneasy giggle at the euphemism. *Patient*—as though the executioner were a doctor. The final cure for all ills.

Abruptly he imagined himself the executioner's victim (*patient*, Charles), kneeling in a pile of straw, neck bared, awaiting the blow, and the breath seemed to freeze in his lungs.

"You swing the sword about, from high above," his father continued: "like this, high above your shoulder, to get up the speed, and then you must aim just right—"

Awaiting the blow, he thought, *blindfolded, hands tied behind you...your heart would race and your breath would come quick and shallow, wouldn't it?*

With an effort Charles balled his fists, closed his eyes for an instant, and turned to face his father, who continued in his usual composed, distant tones.

"—so it passes straight through his neck. It requires strength, control, a keen eye, and steady nerves. You need to know how to do it, and you're strong enough now, I'd judge, to begin practicing with a blade. Only practice will make you skilled at it."

Charles swallowed, glancing covertly at this stranger who was talking so dispassionately about instruments of judicial death and how to use them, this sudden stranger who had once been his father. "I couldn't do that."

"Do..."

"I couldn't ever cut somebody's head off."

"I thought so, too, when I was fourteen." Jean-Baptiste laid the sword back in its crate. He rested a hand, for an instant, on Charles's shoulder. Providence had been kind to him, he went on; in all his career, he'd never yet been ordered to behead anyone.

"But should such an unhappy occasion arise, I'm prepared, both in body—to strike a clean blow—and spiritually, as the law's most terrible servant, to take another's life in the name of the law. Fortunately," he added, "we live in a civilized age; the gentry rarely commit capital offenses."

"The gentry?"

"Only people of noble birth are allowed to be beheaded," Jean-Baptiste reminded him, as he shut the crate and secured it with a small padlock wrought—incongruously enough—into an ornate heart. "Always be sure the swords are locked away. I have two here—this one and a spare. The Parlement gave them to my grandfather, sixty years ago, when he assumed the Paris title. They cost six hundred livres each, back in his day, and I hate to think what it would cost now to replace them."

Charles nodded, impressed. Six hundred livres was more than the average workman earned in a year.

Jean-Baptiste gestured him out to the sunshine of the stable-yard, muddy from the spring rain. "Only nobles may be beheaded," he repeated, as he fished out his keys, "and you must know how to do it yourself, because they have the privilege of being executed by someone of equivalent rank."

Charles frowned. What was he missing? "Another nobleman?"

"If you find studying the criminal law as tedious as I did when I was your age," Jean-Baptiste said dryly, "you should at least read your history." He locked the shed and joined Charles. "Not another nobleman, no, but nearly so. Only the master executioner may behead an aristocrat."

Only the master executioner, he went on, an indispensable functionary of the high court, who held the royal office and title from the Parlement of Paris—grandly, *Maître des Hautes Œuvres*, Master of High Works—could carry out such a solemn duty; he couldn't delegate it to his lackeys as they did with plebeian hangings.

"And you, as my eldest son, will someday hold the Paris title and you may, one day, be less fortunate than I and have to put someone to death with your own hands, so—"

"Father? Why are nobles beheaded while ordinary people are hanged?"

"Decapitation is a privilege, Charles. It illustrates the distinction between the high-born and the common masses. It's an honorable way to die, suitable for a gentleman or gentlewoman."

"Even one who's committed a crime?"

Assault, murder, rebellion, treason, even those?

"Yes, even one who's gone astray and committed some act that's worthy of death. Noble birth implies a tradition of duty and honor, just like our own—and so it's a gentleman's duty, when condemned to die, to hold himself up courageously and maintain the honor of his family name by awaiting the blow without flinching. Ordinary criminals wouldn't have the nerve for it. The dregs of the streets and the slums, they have no noble name or family honor to uphold.

"Imagine," Jean-Baptiste continued, "a common housebreaker, a cutpurse, a brigand, outlaws and cowards all, having the native courage to hold himself still on the scaffold even for a moment or two, while the executioner concentrates on his aim! He'd most likely struggle, or tremble, or even collapse. And that, of course, would spoil the headsman's aim and lead to frightful accidents. It's really to their benefit that the riffraff are hanged."

Charles looked away, feeling a little sick to his stomach, as he usually did when he had to pass the local abattoir on the way to Mass at Saint-Laurent. Its pervasive ooze of filth and stinking stale blood invariably slimed the cobbles and his shoes. If he disliked the thought of innocent animals being slaughtered and butchered nearby for his family's table, how much more repugnant was the prospect of putting human beings to death?

Since his twelfth birthday he'd witnessed at least a dozen executions at Jean-Baptiste's side. *To learn your business*, his father had said. Hanging was humiliating for the victim and Charles had found it unpleasant to watch, but it was reliable, predictable, and passably quick; it was supposed, Jean-Baptiste told him, to snap the neck at once and finish the culprit. If he or she instead strangled to death at the end of the rope, slowly choking while evacuating bladder and bowels, to the mingled amusement, disgust, and indignation of the watching crowds, the executioner's lackeys hadn't done their job properly.

The spring sun was warm on his face. He drew a deep breath, glad to get away from the shed—the one kept locked, where his father kept the tools of his profession, where the children were forbidden to venture—and resolved to light a candle to the Blessed Virgin and pray that he, too, would never have to behead anyone.

"It's a fine afternoon," Jean-Baptiste said. He glanced up at the cloudless sky. "Perhaps we should begin today. You'll start with the dummy sword and get your arms used to supporting the weight at the proper—"

"I'd rather learn about your laboratory," Charles said hastily, eager to examine the rows of dusty bottles and vials, and trying not to think about the executioner's sword at all. "I'd like to learn about medicine and—and curing people." Despite his profession that was both the honor and the curse of the Sanson family, Jean-Baptiste was well known in their outlying parish as a skilled healer, like his father and grandfather before him, with as much expertise in doctoring as many physicians with university degrees.

Jean-Baptiste eyed him for a moment. "How are you getting along with your studies?"

Charles could predict to a hair's breadth that Père Grisel, his tutor, had reported that young Monsieur Sanson had quite a thirst for knowledge, but was an abysmal speller, wrote a poor hand, and had faulty Latin.

"I try my best at Latin. And I know I can't spell. But I like to read anything I can. Natural philosophy, herbalism, anatomy—"

"You're not to spend all your time with those at the expense of history and law."

"No, Father."

Jean-Baptiste's tone was stern, but Charles could tell from a fraction of a smile on his father's lips that he was not altogether displeased with his son's love of learning, whatever branches of knowledge he might be overlooking.

"But I do want to read your scientific books, and learn about medicine."

Jean-Baptiste slipped the key to the shed into his pocket and extracted another. "I see you won't be dissuaded. Very well; the laboratory now, then the wooden sword this afternoon, and no arguments."

Charles grinned and followed him, barely concealing his excitement. Beneath the broad skylight the laboratory was full of mysteries and wonders: a cupboard that held dozens of bottles and small ceramic pots, full of tinctures, syrups, ointments; a shelf of unfamiliar books on botany and anatomy; a brazier for simmering mixtures; and enough mortars and jars of dried herbs to fill an apothecary's shop. Jean-Baptiste pointed at the various articles, explaining, as Charles stared.

A question he'd longed to ask for some years, but had never dared to bring up, hovered at the edge of his memory. Naturally the executioner had frequent contact with corpses. And Jérôme, Jean-Baptiste's chief assistant, a veteran of thirty-five years or more in the profession, had sworn many times that the salve his master prepared would cure anything.

He *would* ask him, for once and for all, when they completed the tour of the outbuilding.

"Father, Jérôme says you know how to make a magic ointment out of hanged men's fat."

He half expected a box on the ear to curb his inquisitiveness, but Jean-Baptiste merely frowned. "Do you believe all the tall tales the servants tell you?"

"Well…no."

"Remember, they're not of our class and they haven't had your education."

"It's not true, then?"

It was an ancient superstition, Jean-Baptiste patiently explained, hundreds of years old, that the executioner could mix a magical salve from dead men's fat. Perhaps Sanson the First and his predecessors in the profession, back in less scientific and enlightened centuries, had concocted such a mixture. But he, Jean-Baptiste Sanson, let the men believe such foolishness only because all ignorant people believed it, and wouldn't be convinced otherwise.

"This is the eighteenth century, not the fourteenth, and I won't have you swallowing such nonsense. It's no different from the old wives' tale about a piece of hangman's rope, or a hanged man's bone, bringing good luck. Pagan superstition, not reason."

"But is there a salve—"

"Yes, I prepare one that soothes skin afflictions and small wounds. They all ask me for it, as I'm sure they asked your grandfather and great-grandfather in their time; they believe it'll cure anything ailing them." He retrieved a ceramic jar from a shelf and pulled out the stopper. "But the salve is made from lard mixed with thyme, myrtle, and a few other medicinal herbs: nothing more."

Charles wrinkled his nose at the pungent odor of bitter herbs mingled with pig fat, worse than the rancid reek of cheap tallow candles that smelled like a soap boiler's back alley, and Jean-Baptiste gave him another of his rare smiles. "It does stink to high heaven."

"So you don't take hanged men's fat?"

"Listen to me." He turned Charles around with a firm grip on his shoulder, so that they were face-to-face. "I would never take the fat of a man for such a thing. Never. It's against God's laws to tamper with a human body."

"But don't you dissect bodies?"

"Yes," Jean-Baptiste admitted, "I look inside criminals' dead bodies to see how God created us, so I can understand better how to heal people. So did your grandfather and great-grandfather. But cooking human flesh to render fat for a charm would be much more repugnant to Him. I wouldn't use even a criminal's body for such a purpose; I'm a man of science, not superstition.

"Though a physician from the university," he added, a trace of scorn in his voice, "wouldn't think of touching a corpse himself, even to instruct his students." In the medical schools, he'd been told, the lecturer stood no nearer to the dissection table than necessary to demonstrate with a long pointer, while some grimy-handed minion in a leather apron did the cutting and the pinning.

He left it unsaid, but Charles understood: The executioner could indulge in no such fastidious snobbery.

"The body of the man we hanged on Tuesday is still here. He has a malformed arm. Would you like to see?"

They would have to send him off for burial soon, if the weather stayed warm. Charles nodded. Fresh corpses weren't particularly dreadful; he'd seen them often enough at the gallows. Though religious law forbade dissection of human corpses, the bodies of the executed were an exception; by their crimes they had forfeited the privilege and blessing that all good, law-abiding Christians could claim, burial in consecrated ground. The executioner had the right to the body, clothes, and effects of his victim—*patient*—for his own profit, and could sell cadavers to the medical school if he pleased, or examine them himself.

Jean-Baptiste unlocked a further door at the rear of the laboratory, which led to a room with another north-facing skylight. Something lay covered on a table in the center. He pulled away the sheet. "See here?"

He had already begun to dissect the man's arm; Charles could see how the muscles were laid out and how the bones beneath were crooked. "I expect he broke his arm when he was a child, and it wasn't set properly," Jean-Baptiste continued.

It wasn't horrid at all, but fascinating. Jean-Baptiste knew how to set bones, among many other useful skills more appropriate to a doctor than an executioner.

I'd like to be able to do that, to be like him, Charles thought; and hastily thrust away the image of his father's sword, the headsman's sword that had belonged to three generations of Sansons and someday would belong to him as it had to his forefathers, forever and ever, time without end, amen.

The Executioner's Heir:
A Novel of Eighteenth-Century France

Susanne Alleyn

eBook, 2013 • US $4.99

Trade paperback, 2013 • $14.99